Welcome to the EVERYTHING® series!

THESE HANDY, accessible books give you all you need to tackle a difficult project, gain a new hobby, comprehend a fascinating topic, prepare for an exam, or even brush up on something you learned back in school but have since forgotten.

You can read an *EVERYTHING*® book from cover to cover or just pick out the information you want from our four useful boxes: e-facts, e-ssentials, e-alerts, and e-questions. We literally give you everything you need to know on the subject, but throw in a lot of fun stuff along the way, too.

We now have well over 300 *EVERYTHING*® books in print, spanning such wide-ranging topics as weddings, pregnancy, wine, learning guitar, one-pot cooking, managing people, and so much more. When you're done reading them all, you can finally say you know *EVERYTHING*®!

Ⓔ Facts: Important sound bytes of information

Ⓔ Essentials: Quick and handy tips

Ⓔ Alerts!: Urgent warnings

Ⓔ Questions?: Solutions to common problems

THE

EVERYTHING.
Series

Dear Reader,

Are you looking to work your mind in new and interesting ways? Do you enjoy playing mind-bending games and solving puzzles? Do you need an interesting activity for an upcoming party? I wrote this lateral thinking puzzle book for your enjoyment and also as a way to push your thought process to its limit, and then break through that boundary. As you solve these lateral thinking puzzles and revel in the solutions, you'll continue to teach yourself to think outside of the box. These puzzles are a great way to pass the hours on a road trip, or spark some fun conversation at your next gathering.

Lateral thinking puzzles are often best solved using a dialogue format with one or more other players. Someone will be the puzzle-giver, and the remaining players will ask yes/no questions to arrive at the correct solution. You will need to employ lateral thinking techniques when you exhaust one line of questioning without determining the correct solution.

In this book you will find lateral thinking puzzles on many different topics, ranging from urban legends to obscure facts to inventions. Some of the puzzles will be quick solves, while others will give you a chance to maximize your brainpower. Each puzzle offers two clues to assist you, in case you get stuck or find yourself on the wrong path to a solution. Good luck and happy solving!

Nikki Katz

THE
EVERYTHING®
LATERAL THINKING PUZZLES BOOK

Hundreds of puzzles to help
you think outside the box

Nikki Katz

Adams Media
Avon, Massachusetts

To my mom and dad.

• • •

An Everything® Series Book.
Everything® and everything.com® are registered trademarks of
F+W Publications, Inc.

Published by Adams Media, an F+W Publications Company
57 Littlefield Street, Avon, MA 02322 U.S.A.
www.adamsmedia.com

ISBN: 1-59337-547-6

Printed in Canada.

J I H G F E D C B A

This publication is designed to provide accurate and authoritative information
with regard to the subject matter covered. It is sold with the understanding that
the publisher is not engaged in rendering legal, accounting, or other professional
advice. If legal advice or other expert assistance is required, the services of a com-
petent professional person should be sought.

—From a *Declaration of Principles* jointly adopted by a Committee of the
American Bar Association and a Committee of Publishers and Associations

Many of the designations used by manufacturers and sellers to distinguish their
product are claimed as trademarks. Where those designations appear in this book
and Adams Media was aware of a trademark claim, the designations have been
printed with initial capital letters.

*This book is available at quantity discounts for bulk purchases.
For information, please call 1-800-872-5627.*

THE

EDITORIAL

Publishing Director: Gary M. Krebs

Associate Managing Editor: Laura M. Daly

Associate Copy Chief: Brett Palana-Shanahan

Acquisitions Editor: Gina Chaimanis

Development Editor: Katie McDonough

Associate Production Editor: Casey Ebert

PRODUCTION

Director of Manufacturing: Susan Beale

Associate Director of Production: Michelle Roy Kelly

Cover Design: Paul Beatrice,
Erick DaCosta, and Matt LeBlanc

Design and Layout: Colleen Cunningham,
Holly Curtis, Sorae Lee

Series Cover Artist: Barry Littmann

Visit the entire Everything® series at www.everything.com

Acknowledgments

Thank you to my agent, Barb Doyen, at Doyen and Doyen Literary Services, Inc., for the chance to complete a third book with Adams Media! Many thanks to the multiple editors I worked with at Adams Media, including Gina Chaimanis.

I'd also like to extend a thank you to everyone who sent me ideas and stories for puzzles, including (in alphabetical order) Amy C., Barb and Paul L., Jayne M., Kristin H., Nicole K., Sharon E., and my husband, Jason. My daughters were fabulous, as always, allowing me to get my work done on schedule. And to everyone whom I cannot thank personally: Thank you for your support and assistance. I hope you can solve all of these puzzles!

Contents

Chapter 1
Warm-up Puzzles

A re you new to the world of lateral thinking puzzles, or do you need a quick refresher on the concepts? If so, this chapter is for you. The puzzles given here are a great warm-up for the more challenging puzzles in the remainder of the book. With these basic logic problems, you'll learn to test your initial assumptions and begin to search for other possible answers. The clues are quickly available to assist you, but give yourself a chance to solve the puzzles without help first.

Puzzle 1-1
George walked in the door and said to his wife, "I shot two eagles today." She sighed and told him he should have been able to shoot more. Why wasn't she upset that he shot an endangered species?

Clues: 1. George normally shoots in grassy areas. 2. George wears special shoes.

Puzzle 1-2
When the boy told his mother he was going to join the band, she became very upset and suspected bad things were going to happen. Why?

Clues: 1. She didn't like the type of music he listened to. 2. He did not disclose the name of the band.

Puzzle 1-3
The amateur golf player was able to hit a hole-in-one on four of the eighteen holes. How?

Clues: 1. He was playing with his family. 2. The course was short.

Puzzle 1-4
She lived on Campus but had never attended college. Why?

Clues: 1. Others on Campus had not attended college either. 2. The school was not close by.

Puzzle 1-5
Her windshield did not get wet, although it was raining all around her.

Clues: 1. She was sitting in the driver's seat of her car. 2. She could see the rain at a close distance.

Puzzle 1-6
Catherine was startled and dropped her full cup on the floor. Not one person in the room reacted. Why?

Clues: 1. People saw her drop the drink, but didn't react. 2. The drink did not spill.

Puzzle 1-7
He saw the stop sign, but did not stop his automobile. Why?

Clues: 1. He was driving the car. 2. There were other vehicles around who did stop.

Puzzle 1-8
Kelly is in her sophomore year of college when she celebrates her fifth birthday. How?

Clues: 1. She looks older than five. 2. She often celebrates other birthdays.

Puzzle 1-9

Jana's daughter Maria came into the kitchen saying Daddy wanted a drink. Jana handed her a full glass. Three minutes later Maria came in again with the same request. A few minutes later Daddy walked in with an angry look on his face. Why?

Clues: 1. Daddy had asked for the drink. 2. The child was being manipulative.

Puzzle 1-10

The young boy kept getting his dates confused, especially the months of September, October, November, and December. Why?

Clues: 1. He was using his own system for remembering them. 2. He liked to write out the months using numbers.

 *Question?*

So what is a lateral thinking puzzle anyway?

The basic idea of a lateral thinking puzzle is that there exists a puzzle, or problem, with a solution that requires you to think in a different way than you normally would—you must think *laterally*. Lateral thinking teaches you to check any assumptions you might have made about the situation being discussed.

Puzzle 1-11
She told the maid to stop washing the windows in the dining room. Why?

Clues: 1. The maid washed them every week. 2. She did a fabulous job, leaving no streaks behind.

Puzzle 1-12
Marcia received Barbie dolls from all of her friends, even though her name wasn't Barb and she was petite with brown hair. Why did they give them to her?

Clues: 1. The dolls were a gift for her birthday. 2. She was an adult.

Puzzle 1-13
She drove around the neighborhood for twenty-five minutes before pulling into her driveway. Why?

Clues: 1. She was not alone in the vehicle. 2. She was not early arriving home.

Puzzle 1-14
He was taller than his date, but he still wore shoes with high heels. Why?

Clues: 1. He was keeping with the fashion. 2. His date wore high heels as well.

Puzzle 1-15
When the driver lost control of the car, the passenger was able to stop the vehicle without moving from his seat. How?

Clues: 1. The passenger did not reach over to guide the steering wheel. 2. The two were not playing a video game.

Puzzle 1-16
George drove through the building, but nobody was hurt and no damage to the structure occurred. How?

Clues: 1. He was not playing golf. 2. George was driving a vehicle.

Puzzle 1-17
Kathleen called for an ambulance even though she was perfectly capable of driving to the hospital herself. Explain.

Clues: 1. A car was available to her. 2. She was not afraid of driving.

Puzzle 1-18
She desperately wanted that drink but just couldn't seem to reach it. Why?

Clues: 1. She kept moving toward it. 2. She was not contained in any way.

Puzzle 1-19
The little boy never chewed gum, but one day his father took the little boy out of his seat and found a piece of gum stuck in his hair. What happened?

Clues: 1. Nobody else was around. 2. The father had been chewing gum.

Puzzle 1-20
A bird flaps his wings, traveling a thousand miles, with his cage around him. How?

Clues: 1. The bird does not live in an atrium. 2. The bird is alive.

Puzzle 1-21
Casey took three small steps, one large step, four small steps, and one last large step. Why?

Clues: 1. She purposely spaced out her steps. 2. She was not stepping over anything.

Puzzle 1-22
She knew the plain white envelope with no writing contained a love note. How?

Clues: 1. She could not tell whom the envelope was from. 2. She received multiple notes that day.

Puzzle 1-23

Your mom's cousin is married and has five sons. Each son has one sister. How many people are in the family?

Clues: 1. Don't add extra people. 2. Your mom is not part of the family.

Puzzle 1-24

How much dirt is in a square hole, 4 inches on each side and 8 inches deep?

Clues: 1. The volume is important. 2. It could have been filled with water.

Puzzle 1-25

A baby is in the same room as her parents. She hiccups for five minutes but the parents don't hear anything.

Clues: 1. The parents are not deaf. 2. They can see the movement of the hiccups, but cannot hear it.

Puzzle 1-26

Although Henry suffered from arachnophobia, he did not scream when he found a large spider on his doorstep that evening. Why?

Clues: 1. It was alive. 2. It was not a model of car.

Puzzle 1-27

A mother was cleaning up her son's room when she stumbled across a book. Without even opening it to see what was inside, she called her husband and told him to locate their son immediately. Why?

Clues: 1. The title of the book was frightening. 2. Her son had been despondent lately.

Puzzle 1-28

The thief returned to the scene of the crime, but he didn't steal anything. He stayed there for over an hour, and was not interrupted. What happened?

Clues: 1. He brought something with him. 2. He was new to the profession.

 Alert!

> In some of the puzzles you might find that there is extraneous information given to you that is not necessary to determine the solution. This tactic is designed to put you on the wrong track, while at the same time teaching you how to weed out facts that are unrelated to the topic at hand.

Puzzle 1-29

When her son was born, Christy had a strong sense that he was going to be left-handed. She was correct. How did she know?

Clues: 1. Nobody in her family was left-handed. 2. Her son was not favoring his left hand.

Puzzle 1-30

Even though he was picked as man of the year, nobody wanted to date him. Why?

Clues: 1. It was a prestigious magazine that chose him as the honest winner. 2. Women just thought he was too cold.

Puzzle 1-31

He was arrested after he couldn't come up with the full $4.00 fee at the tollbooth. Why?

Clues: 1. He was not prepared to pay the toll. 2. He was driving an automobile.

Puzzle 1-32

She did not take it as a compliment when he said she smelled like a flower. Why?

Clues: 1. He did not say she smelled like a rose. 2. She knew he did not like her.

Puzzle 1-33
Even though she and her husband were happily married, Tanya did not list her diamond wedding band as part of her assets. Why?

Clues: 1. She did not worry about it being stolen. 2. She was about to have everything important taken away.

Puzzle 1-34
He quickly typed out a message even thought it didn't mean anything. Why?

Clues: 1. The message had significance, but the actual text did not stand for anything. 2. He was hoping for a response.

Puzzle 1-35
If the mother had 206 bones in her body, how many did her daughter have?

Clues: 1. Her daughter was born completely healthy with no abnormalities. 2. Her daughter did not have the same amount of bones as she did.

Puzzle 1-36
The twin girls went to visit their parents' gravesite each year on the anniversary of the car crash, even though nobody was buried inside. Why did they go?

Clues: 1. Their parents had died in the car crash. 2. They stood in the shadow of the tomb and scattered flowers.

Puzzle 1-37
Although everyone knows his name and what he looks like, they wouldn't be able to pick his picture out of a group. Why?

Clues: 1. They would not be able to identify his features. 2. His image exists in many people's homes.

Puzzle 1-38
The man pulled a sword out of its sheath and held it up as a request to duel with his enemy. Before he took two steps forward, he fell over and died. What happened?

Clues: 1. His enemy killed him. 2. This did not take place in ancient Europe.

Puzzle 1-39
He named his dog after a common characteristic associated with the pet. What was it?

Clues: 1. He didn't know originally that he was naming his dog for this word. 2. He just picked a common name.

Puzzle 1-40
She raced with her dog around the hot spots of Atlantic City in under 20 minutes. How?

Clues: 1. She was not out of breath after the run. 2. She stopped at least five times along the route.

Puzzle 1-41
The manufacturers decided they wanted to cut back on the shipping costs of their product, so what did they do?

Clues: 1. This is a based on a true event. 2. They found a way to shrink the product significantly.

Puzzle 1-42
A couple living in Montana were planning their first trip to Paris. The husband wanted to travel by plane but his wife wanted to travel by train. The wife won the argument. How?

Clues: 1. She was afraid to fly. 2. The train was a much more economical choice.

Puzzle 1-43
Catherine stepped out of the elevator and into her office. She was talking on her cellular phone as she passed her administrative assistant, Mike. She covered the mouth-piece and mouthed that she was talking to an important client. How did Mike know that she was lying?

Clues: 1. Catherine gave the name of a specific client. 2. She was over an hour late arriving at the office.

Puzzle 1-44

When getting his change back from a purchase, a man asked the merchant for half of a quarter. What did the merchant do?

Clues: 1. The merchant was very agreeable in coming up with a solution. 2. The customer received his correct change and was on his way.

Puzzle 1-45

Jake and Cathy brought home their newborn and laid her down in her bassinet. Jake quickly left the room and came back in carrying his first gift for the baby girl. Cathy crossed her fingers behind her back and hoped it wouldn't work. Why?

Clues: 1. She thought it was a nice gesture, but she liked the second option better. 2. It was not a loud, annoying toy.

Puzzle 1-46

Keri was startled in the middle of the night. She got up and ran headfirst into her door. Why didn't she pay attention to where she was going?

Clues: 1. She was hardly awake. 2. She was awakened by a very loud noise.

Puzzle 1-47
Jennifer and Kyle wanted to visit Vermont for the Equinox. They decided to go in July. How is that possible?

Clues: 1. They knew when the spring and winter Equinoxes occur. 2. They were not visiting a museum or photography exhibit.

Puzzle 1-48
Carmen repeatedly tried to light the candle in the dark room. After she finally got it lit, she looked up and immediately blew it out. Why?

Clues: 1. She was not afraid of what she saw in the dim glow of the candle. 2. She did not use the candle to look for something.

Puzzle 1-49
Theresa started singing and the class bully tripped. Why?

Clues: 1. She did not have a horrible voice. 2. She did not tell anyone to trip the bully.

Puzzle 1-50
A boy plays on the edge of the beach and looks at the water from time to time, hoping to see a surfer in the ocean. He leaves a few hours later, disappointed. Why?

Clues: 1. He sees people playing in the water, but nobody is surfing. 2. His mother didn't clarify where they were going.

Puzzle 1-51
Bob threw an object through his neighbor's window, but the neighbor didn't mind. Why?

Clues: 1. Bob was trying to protect his neighbor. 2. He was not attempting to wake him in the middle of the night.

Puzzle 1-52
Joyce got a kiss from her boss, but she wasn't upset and she didn't press charges. Why?

Clues: 1. They were not dating. 2. Joyce did not find the gesture very romantic.

Puzzle 1-53
Harold opened up the package and became distressed. He dug a hole, placed the package in it, and went inside. Why?

Clues: 1. He did not throw it down in anger. 2. The package ultimately belonged in the ground.

Puzzle 1-54
Stacy fell into the swimming pool and everyone around her knew she died. Nobody tried to save her. Why?

Clues: 1. She did not drown in the water. 2. She was fully clothed.

Puzzle 1-55
When Charlie's neighbors moved away, his house went up in value. Why?

Clues: 1. They were not homeowners. 2. The neighbors were a bit smelly.

Puzzle 1-56
The birds were alive but remained in the same place, year after year. Why?

Clues: 1. They were not in a cage. 2. They did not have their wings clipped.

Puzzle 1-57
The man was making strange noises when a stranger shot him in the leg. Why did the injured man not press charges?

Clues: 1. The police investigated the shooting and called it accidental. 2. The injured man was hospitalized for a while.

 Essential

> In many puzzles, there are one or two key elements of the scenario that are left out of the description. Sometimes those elements are given to you in the clues, but if you choose not to read the clues or the information is unavailable, you will have to think outside your traditional scope of ideas to find the solution.

Puzzle 1-58

Luke's superior officer told him to remove the pile of bricks. After completing the task he was demoted. Why?

Clues: 1. He didn't follow the orders correctly. 2. He did not pick up the bricks himself; rather, he delegated it.

Puzzle 1-59

He was shocked to learn that a deformed product was even more expensive than one that was without flaws. What was he looking to buy?

Clues: 1. The deformed object was more rare than perfect ones. 2. His girlfriend was not around at the time.

Puzzle 1-60

Shauna went to an ice-cream parlor with several of her friends. They asked her what flavor she wanted and she told them that it didn't matter because she couldn't tell the difference. Why?

Clues: 1. She could eat food as normal. 2. She did not have sinus or allergy problems.

Chapter 2
Why Did That Happen?

trange situations, bizarre occurrences, misunderstood intentions, and unforeseeable circumstances: these are the incidents that make up the puzzles in this chapter. Your task is to figure out why something happened or why someone acted in the manner he did. When you solve these puzzles you'll need to check your assumptions, specifically when it comes to the who, what, when, where, and why of the information you are given. You'll need to be flexible and creative to reach the correct solution.

Puzzle 2-1
A woman calls her husband at work to tell him that one of the chairs is wet. He immediately hangs up the phone and leaves the office. Why?

Clues: 1. The husband is heading to pick up his wife. 2. The woman did not spill a drink on the chair.

Puzzle 2-2
A woman receives a phone call from her daughter but she doesn't recognize her voice. Why?

Clues: 1. The woman was not expecting the phone call from her daughter. 2. The daughter did not have laryngitis, and she wasn't trying to disguise her voice.

Puzzle 2-3
A woman hears the oven beep and starts crying. Why?

Clues: 1. The woman was not expecting to hear the oven beep. 2. Any sound would have caused the woman to cry.

Puzzle 2-4
A woman living in Florida looked out her window and spotted a blue convertible on the sand. The vehicle was about to be swallowed by waves as the tide continued to come in. She called the police, but when they arrived, they were not alarmed. Why?

Clues: 1. They were eventually able to find the car. 2. Nobody was in any danger of drowning.

Puzzle 2-5
The power went out, and he decided to take a bath. He went up to the bathroom, but he couldn't add any water to the bathtub. Why?

Clues: 1. The water was not turned off. 2. There was plenty of hot water.

Puzzle 2-6
Christopher turned as the door opened and saw Amelia standing there. Frightened, he ran to the edge of the porch and jumped, landing three stories below. He stood, unharmed, and continued running. How?

Clues: 1. He jumped off high objects often. 2. Christopher and Amelia were unrelated.

Puzzle 2-7
A man is shoved into the trunk of a car and locked inside. When he is finally rescued and taken to the hospital, the police arrive to arrest him. Why?

Clues: 1. He did not damage the trunk from inside. 2. He was not in the trunk with a dead body.

Puzzle 2-8

Tyler was walking down the street and kept hearing a strange noise. He turned to look around, but could not determine where it was coming from. Nobody else appeared to hear the noise. Why?

Clues: 1. Tyler was not walking down the street alone. 2. He never determined the source of the sound.

Puzzle 2-9

Charles arrived in town with his Mustang, stopped only once to let a woman cross the street, and left the town with his Mercedes. How?

Clues: 1. He did not get out of a car. 2. He did not have any passengers.

Puzzle 2-10

She was obsessed with keeping her house clean, but her husband always offered to do a couple of chores each day. Why?

Clues: 1. She would rather have done them herself, but for the hassle. 2. They were not outdoor chores.

Puzzle 2-11

The Smith family's neighbor learned a lot about them while they were gone on vacation. How?

Clues: 1. He did not read their mail. 2. He did not intentionally spy on them, but could see into their house rather easily.

Fact

> Many of the puzzles that are included in this chapter
> arose from real-life news stories and articles. The strange
> circumstances that people find themselves in can evolve
> into lateral thinking situations by leaving out key pieces of
> information or by placing the event in a different setting.

Puzzle 2-12

A chef was cleaning the freezer of his restaurant when he
moved a cloth. A large spider bit him on the hand. Shortly
afterward he was dizzy and his hand was swelling at a
rapid rate. His colleague rushed him to the hospital. He
had no idea what type of spider bit him, so how did the
doctors determine how to treat it?

Clues: 1. He was somehow able to provide a description
of the spider even though he could not speak. 2. The doctors could not tell from the appearance of the wound.

Puzzle 2-13

The grandfather opened the door after winning the local
golf tournament to find a police officer on his porch, ready
to arrest him. Why?

Clues: 1. The police officer assumed something that was
untrue. 2. After clearing up the misunderstanding, all
charges were dropped.

Puzzle 2-14

A girl and her friend were talking in a restaurant about the party they had been to the weekend before. Later that week, the girl was fined a large amount of money. Why?

Clues: 1. She had done nothing wrong at the party. 2. She was overheard talking about someone at the party.

Puzzle 2-15

The woman opened the door and was handed a bouquet of roses from a local florist. She went inside and opened the card, and it was from her husband for Valentine's Day. She immediately began to cry. Why?

Clues: 1. She did not cry tears of joy. 2. The husband and wife were not separated.

Puzzle 2-16

The company bought insurance before their annual get-together. They weren't afraid of health hazards or any of the employees damaging the facilities, so why did they purchase insurance?

Clues: 1. They were hosting a tournament. 2. They were offering incentive prizes.

Puzzle 2-17
The man used his car to block a truck from entering a highway. Why was the driver of the truck arrested and not the man who caused the accident?

Clues: 1. The car used to block the truck was not a police car. 2. The truck driver was unable to stop his truck.

Puzzle 2-18
Although the couple saw many animals on the safari, they were angry and demanded a refund. Why?

Clues: 1. It was not an African safari. 2. They were expecting to see different animals.

Puzzle 2-19
Timothy looked out the window and watched as the weather changed rapidly from sunny and warm, to snowing, to raining and gusty. How?

Clues: 1. It was night. 2. He could hear the weather being discussed.

Puzzle 2-20
His mother wasn't against tattoos, but she was upset when he got one. Why?

Clues: 1. She was upset at what it said. 2. The tattoo was not offensive in any way.

Puzzle 2-21

The two men spent hours drilling a hole into the restroom. They were not attempting to spy on anyone, so why did they do it?

Clues: 1. They did not want a hole into the restroom. 2. They were not trying to escape.

Puzzle 2-22

She went to the gym and the employees called an ambulance. Why?

Clues: 1. She did not become injured from any of the equipment. 2. She did not pass out.

Puzzle 2-23

It was March 16th and she cried until April. Why?

Clues: 1. She didn't cry after April. 2. She needed some comforting.

 *Question?*

Why aren't multiple solutions given for these puzzles?
The puzzles in this book offer you a scenario, of which there may be multiple solutions. Although you may like your solution better, or there may be another viable answer, you are looking for the solution listed in the back of the book, which is designed to be surprising and interesting.

Puzzle 2-24

She began to wonder if her nephew suffered from some type of disorder. Why?

Clues: 1. He was randomly calling out names. 2. She couldn't see what he was doing.

Puzzle 2-25

As he exited the store, he accidentally dropped some money. He didn't bother to pick it up. Why?

Clues: 1. He didn't want to appear cheap. 2. He knew somebody else would benefit from the money.

Puzzle 2-26

Although the house was only a few miles away, he bought it without viewing it. Why?

Clues: 1. There were no other houses in the area that were similar that he could view. 2. He was in no hurry to move in.

Puzzle 2-27

The knights continued to chase each other around, but the gap between them never closed. Why?

Clues: 1. They were equal distances apart. 2. They never tired of riding around.

Puzzle 2-28

Casey wanted her new boyfriend to gain some weight. She thought his current weight was unhealthy, but she knew he was stressed and needed some help. She bought him a gift and took it by the office. He quickly crumbled to the floor. Why?

Clues: 1. He hadn't disclosed all of his health information. 2. He thanked her for the gift before falling down.

Puzzle 2-29

Although he was extremely quiet and polite, Chad was still asked to leave the library. Why?

Clues: 1. He was not homeless. 2. He was bothering a few of the patrons.

Puzzle 2-30

After a night of partying with her friends, Patti arrived home wearing new jewelry. Her boyfriend was visibly upset. Why?

Clues: 1. Someone else gave her the jewelry. 2. He forgot what event she went out to celebrate.

Puzzle 2-31

He bought his wife an expensive gold necklace, but she asked for a divorce anyway. Why?

Clues: 1. The necklace was a surprise. 2. She was not upset prior to receiving the gift.

Puzzle 2-32
Kylie visited a boutique market and bought decorations, a sanitizer, a stain remover, a whitener, sore throat relief, and some food, all for under $2.00. How?

Clues: 1. She did not use coupons. 2. She bought only three items.

Puzzle 2-33
She removed the blindfold from her date as they sat down for dinner and he began to hyperventilate. Why?

Clues: 1. He was not sick. 2. There was no food on the table.

Puzzle 2-34
Sam was on a deserted island. He wasn't rescued, so how did he get off?

Clues: 1. He did not build a boat. 2. He did not swim.

Puzzle 2-35
The wind began blowing and he was arrested shortly thereafter. Why?

Clues: 1. He was not using the wind for any reason (sail, fly a kite, etc.). 2. The wind did not assist him.

Puzzle 2-36

She removed the sugar from her son's diet and he said, "I love you." Why?

Clues: 1. He didn't realize that she was removing the sugar. 2. He had never said "I love you" before.

Puzzle 2-37

Because of his black suit he won $500. Why?

Clues: 1. The suit was not part of a uniform. 2. There was no money in the pocket of the suit.

Puzzle 2-38

Why did the young man forcefully grab the rosary beads out of his mother's hands?

Clues: 1. His mother was not angry with him. 2. He was not angry with his mother.

Puzzle 2-39

An employee of a thrift store sat sifting through receipts looking for a purchase of plastic Easter eggs earlier in the week. Why?

Clues: 1. He had been asked to contact the buyer. 2. The eggs had been left behind by a deceased woman.

Puzzle 2-40

The woman lived by herself in an apartment in New York. Each week she purchased a case of bottled water, but she only drank twelve of the twenty-four bottles. What happened to the other half?

Clues: 1. She did not use them for cooking or cleaning. 2. She did not give them to another person.

Puzzle 2-41

The man urinated on the floor of the public restroom because the toilet was out of order. He was not in any hurry, and there were other restrooms in the building, so why did he go there?

Clues: 1. He misunderstood the directions. 2. He thought nothing of what he had done.

Puzzle 2-42

For one week, each morning a woman went up to her neighbor's house and stuck something through the letter box. It wasn't a letter, so what was it?

Clues: 1. The neighbor was on vacation for a week. 2. The woman attempted to get the local police involved.

Puzzle 2-43

Trenton walked up to the local minimum-security prison and asked to be placed in a cell. Why?

Clues: 1. He knew the prison very well. 2. He was not a psychiatrist.

Puzzle 2-44

The doorbell rang in the middle of the night, but nobody was outside the door. What happened?

Clues: 1. An animal did not ring the doorbell. 2. It wasn't a person running up to the door and hiding.

Puzzle 2-45

It was unfortunate for her that her husband needed crutches. Why?

Clues: 1. She might have been more prepared if she hadn't expected to see him with crutches. 2. Her husband was not happy with her.

ⓔ Alert!

The term "lateral thinking" was created by Edward de Bono and it represents a process and willingness to look at things in different ways. He suggests disrupting your sequence of thinking to arrive at the solution from a different angle. Lateral thinking is the opposite of "vertical thinking."

Puzzle 2-46

After spending all night off the slopes, the two skiers were sent to the hospital for hypothermia. Why?

Clues: 1. They did not leave their windows open. 2. They were wearing thick clothing.

Puzzle 2-47

Jonathan opened up the plain white envelope with no return address. Inside was a birthday card. He knew who sent it without opening the card to read the message inside. How?

Clues: 1. There was no handwriting or stamps on the front of the card. 2. There were no words on the front to indicate it was from a relative.

Puzzle 2-48

After the man was sentenced to a twelve-year jail sentence for hitting Kristine over the head with a beer bottle in a bar, she walked up to him and thanked him. Why?

Clues: 1. Thanks to him she was still alive. 2. He still had to serve time.

Puzzle 2-49

The Humane Society put a hold on selling cats even though they were healthy and desired by patrons. Why?

Clues: 1. They had many animals for sale. 2. They worried about the animals' safety after they were taken.

Puzzle 2-50

Josh wore a surgical mask in public even though he wasn't sick, he didn't have a breathing disorder, and he wasn't paranoid about becoming ill. Why did he wear it?

Clues: 1. He was not making a fashion statement. 2. He wore it often, but only at one location.

Puzzle 2-51

The woman declined the offer of insurance, but she kept a lookout all evening. Why?

Clues: 1. She was worried they might come back. 2. Her neighbors had offered her the insurance.

Puzzle 2-52

An elderly man played the lottery and won, but had to share the winnings with many other people. He didn't know any of them, so why did they win with the same numbers?

Clues: 1. A major newsworthy event had recently occurred. 2. Many people were using the event to dictate their lottery numbers.

Puzzle 2-53
Their mother shipped their Christmas presents ahead of time, but shortly after delivery they were stolen right off their front porch. Why was it lucky for them that the gifts were taken?

Clues: 1. There was nothing wrong with the gifts. 2. Their mother felt guilty that there were no gifts to open.

Puzzle 2-54
The man was prohibited from donating his kidney, even thought it was a match to somebody who needed it. Why?

Clues: 1. He did not have a disease that prevented him from donating the organ. 2. His guardian did not want to allow it.

Puzzle 2-55
The man walked up to the cashier, paid with a credit card, and signed his name. He walked out of the department store and was greeted at his car by a police officer. Why?

Clues: 1. He did not shoplift any other merchandise. 2. He was not easily recognizable as a top criminal.

Puzzle 2-56
The parents were charged with child abuse even though they did not physically or verbally abuse their son. What happened?

Clues: 1. They asked their son to do them a favor. 2. The son was not directly harmed.

Puzzle 2-57
The owner fed her dog a cookie out of the box, and then proceeded to eat one herself. Why?

Clues: 1. She was not ravenous. 2. She did not normally eat her dog's food.

Puzzle 2-58
The man was accused of being a cannibal, but the allegations turned out to be false. What happened?

Clues: 1. He was not seen eating anything peculiar. 2. He was not a murder suspect.

Puzzle 2-59
The new park was an outdoor community center complete with picnic tables, play areas, a swing set, and stages. Why did it remain closed to the public?

Clues: 1. The park was not condemned. 2. The residents of the area wanted to use it.

Chapter 3
Play on Words

Each puzzle in this chapter includes a play on words, but those in the second half (starting with **Puzzle 3-31**) are best suited for a group. Each of the group puzzles contains a homophone—signaled by one word within the question followed by its homophone in parentheses. These puzzles are worded so that when the host reads each one out loud, the listeners will hopefully interpret the problem using the meaning of the homophone in parentheses. In actuality, the correct solution is found when using the homophone outside the parentheses.

Puzzle 3-1
A boy is looking at his new school when he suddenly realizes that all but one will be dead within the week. Why?

Clues: 1. School is not in session 2. The classmates are not compatible.

Puzzle 3-2
The boat broke and their Thanksgiving was ruined. Why?

Clues: 1. They were not traveling by boat. 2. They enjoyed eating dinner together.

Puzzle 3-3
If corn should be grilled for 20 minutes, do you know how long hot dogs should be cooked?

Clues: 1. The time is irrelevant. 2. The hot dogs are grilled as well.

Puzzle 3-4
George, a used car salesman, often earned extra money by cleaning the interiors of the vehicles. One day George's boss asked him to clean the trunks, but he declined. Why?

Clues: 1. He thought it was even more of a dirty job. 2. The trunks were not very old.

Puzzle 3-5
He promised her he would give her a ring on her birthday. She was disappointed when she opened the box. Why?

Clues: 1. There were no jewels involved. 2. She was expecting something with more value.

Puzzle 3-6
Bill's manager yelled at him during spring training after he had two Grand Slams. Why?

Clues: 1. Bill was hungry. 2. Bill was not in very good shape.

Puzzle 3-7
She was extremely upset when her husband got a turkey the day before Thanksgiving, even though she hadn't purchased one for their dinner. Why?

Clues: 1. The size of the turkey was not an issue. 2. She was extremely competitive.

Puzzle 3-8
Many people saw the murder, but not one person attempted to call the police. Why?

Clues: 1. There were no police around. 2. They were not watching it on television or in the movie theater.

Puzzle 3-9

Jon showed up at Andrea's door with a dozen roses and a ring. She was very excited and asked what it meant. He told her that he was sorry for their extensive courtship, he loved her, and he was ready to be committed. Two days later Andrea called the engagement off and threw out the flowers. Why?

Clues: 1. She felt betrayed. 2. He didn't cheat on her.

Puzzle 3-10

He drove for a while, gave up, and went home. Why?

Clues: 1. He was not lost. 2. He did not run out of gas.

Puzzle 3-11

He walked up to the pit, looked down, and saw the mangled bodies inside. He immediately knew the manner in which they had died. How?

Clues: 1. He did not expect to see any survivors. 2. The bodies had been there for a while.

Puzzle 3-12

He arrived at the bottom of the tree and found a dead child. What happened?

Clues: 1. He had known about the child. 2. He had not been looking very long.

Puzzle: 3-13

Although Jonathan longed to play guitar in a band, when his dad suggested he join this one, Jonathan politely declined. Why?

Clues: 1. He was certainly qualified. 2. He didn't think he would get to play the guitar much.

Puzzle 3-14

She loved sugary food, but she was getting sick of cookies. Why?

Clues: 1. She was not in the Girl Scouts. 2. She had not eaten a lot of cookies.

Puzzle 3-15

The priest continued to ask for a blessing until he was finally declared mentally unstable and removed from his position. Why?

Clues: 1. The blessing was an odd request. 2. The blessing is unavailable.

Puzzle 3-16

The teenage boy died while surfing. He did not drown, nor did a shark bite him. What happened?

Clues: 1. He was not anywhere near the water. 2. He was not surfing on the Internet.

Puzzle 3-17

Even though his stomach was rumbling and he was very hungry, Tony did not take anything off the plate. It was full, so why did he wait to eat?

Clues: 1. The plate had been passed to him. 2. Tony put something on the plate but did not take anything off.

Puzzle 3-18

Henry stomped on the plate but it didn't break. Why?

Clues: 1. He came running up and jumped purposely on the plate. 2. He was excited and didn't worry about it breaking.

Puzzle 3-19

Carrie played with a plate that contained a bunch of chewed food. Why didn't it bother her?

Clues: 1. She had chewed up the food. 2. She had gotten used to playing with food.

Puzzle 3-20

She ran into the store on her way home. Why did everyone begin screaming?

Clues: 1. She was not carrying a gun. 2. She did not look menacing or threaten anyone.

Puzzle 3-21

She told her husband about the affair she was having with her coworker, and he ignored her. Why?

Clues: 1. He was still very much in love with his wife. 2. He didn't really care about the affair.

Puzzle 3-22

Lila was playing with her skirt when the bow came untied. Her mother was irate and sent her to her room. Why?

Clues: 1. She was wearing a bathing suit underneath her skirt. 2. She was not paying attention to her surroundings.

Puzzle 3-23

Although Robert was not a procrastinator, he continued to push back his deadline. Why?

Clues: 1. More and more people kept coming to see him. 2. He was not in a hurry to go anywhere.

 **Essential**

Many of these play-on-word puzzles use homographs to confuse you. A homograph is a word that has the same spelling as another but differs in meaning, origin, and, in some cases, pronunciation. As an example, the word bow can be a decorative knot, the front of a ship, or a verb meaning to bend.

Puzzle 3-24

She had a long shower, but when she came out her hair was not wet. How?

Clues: 1. She did not wear a towel or bathing cap. 2. She was not in a bathroom.

Puzzle 3-25

Steven was fired after his first round of boxing. Why?

Clues: 1. He wasn't injured during the round. 2. He didn't lose the match.

Puzzle 3-26

Carli cleaned up the entire house, but her daughter destroyed the majority of rooms with one flick of her wrist. How did she do it?

Clues: 1. Carli was able to clean up the mess relatively quickly. 2. Her daughter swore it was an accident.

Puzzle 3-27

He accidentally bumped his cheek against the nail, but wasn't injured. Why?

Clues: 1. He bumped the nail at a rapid pace. 2. He was aiming for it.

Puzzle 3-28

The parliament talked late into the night without a single member becoming tired. Why?

Clues: 1. They were not having an important discussion. 2. They were not under a deadline.

Puzzle 3-29

The musician was able to use the instrument to save many people's lives. How?

Clues: 1. He was not playing the instrument. 2. Their lives were in danger and they were lucky he was around.

Puzzle 3-30

The detective closed the case, saying that it was a suicide. Why did he later find himself in prison faced with murder charges?

Clues: 1. He had lied about the suicide attempt. 2. He had not fully disclosed all the information he knew.

Puzzle 3-31

His mom insisted that he go to alter (altar) that Sunday, but he was afraid of being punished. Why?

Clues: 1. He had a long trip ahead of him. 2. He had been expelled from of his public school.

Puzzle 3-32

He used his clause (claws) to fight his way through. What happened next?

Clues: 1. He was human. 2. He fought his way through the legal system.

Puzzle 3-33

The parents went to see the auricle (oracle) and were told that nothing was wrong. They were upset at the response. Why?

Clues: 1. They did not want to have to look further. 2. They were hoping that there was a solution.

 Fact

Did you know that in the Hawaiian language, a majority of the words have multiple definitions and often have hidden meanings? Hawaiians understand the correct meaning of the word being spoken based on the context of the sentence or phrase.

Puzzle 3-34

His wife was heartbroken when he came home with the title "barren" (baron).

Clues: 1. She wasn't looking forward to the life ahead of them. 2. She didn't think he deserved it.

Puzzle 3-35

It was a parent (apparent) who ran through the emergency room crying. What happened?

Clues: 1. A little boy lay quietly on a gurney. 2. There were sobs and hysteria.

Puzzle 3-36

Joe walked in with a bin of carets (carrots) from the garden. Even thought it was less than half full, he couldn't believe his luck. Why?

Clues: 1. He had been digging up his garden to plant new seeds. 2. He found the basket.

Puzzle 3-37

The meat was already cooked when he brought it out to the grille (grill). What did he do next?

Clues: 1. He knew everyone was hungry. 2. The food was cooked completely through.

Puzzle 3-38

He wanted to illude (elude) his girlfriend at the jewelry store, so he bought her a piece of costume jewelry. Why?

Clues: 1. She was in the store looking at other jewelry. 2. They had been dating for over two years.

Puzzle 3-39
The little girl sat in the corner at the party and was silent. Her parents later said she was aweful (awful). Why?

Clues: 1. She was usually a very active and entertaining child. 2. She was staring around the room in wonder.

Puzzle 3-40
She wanted to enter the party discretely (discreetly), but she wore her bright red dress and slinky sandals. Why?

Clues: 1. She loved being the center of attention. 2. She was attending the party with her husband.

Puzzle 3-41
The sisters were not concerned when their ant (aunt) began pacing back and forth angrily.

Clues: 1. They did not expect a confrontation. 2. They were purposely provoking their ant.

Puzzle 3-42
Even though she had ridden horses since she was a young adult, she had no idea what to do when the trainer told her to galop (gallop).

Clues: 1. She was taking lessons. 2. She clearly heard the instructor.

Puzzle 3-43

He wanted to halve (have) the picture, but his mother emphatically told him "no." Why?

Clues: 1. The picture had personal significance for him. 2. She wanted to keep it on the wall in her living room.

Puzzle 3-44

At the end of the trial, court reporters claimed that it was his innocents (innocence) that caused the jury to convict him. Why?

Clues: 1. He pleaded "not guilty." 2. He did not testify in the trial.

Puzzle 3-45

She kneaded (needed) to see him that afternoon, so she worked faster than normal. Why?

Clues: 1. She didn't have much time until they got together. 2. She always brought him the same thing.

Puzzle 3-46

They told him to properly dispose of the missals (missiles). His boss didn't care when he threw them in the trash. Why?

Clues: 1. They were not able to cause any danger. 2. They were used.

Puzzle 3-47
The knight (night) fell upon them like a blanket and she knew Jonathan was dead. Why?

Clues: 1. He didn't make a sound. 2. She was afraid for her own life, too.

Puzzle 3-48
The captain at sea kept searching for a peer (pier). He finally found one and made for land. Why?

Clues: 1. He was anxious to get home to his family. 2. He had been searching for over a year.

Puzzle 3-49
Christopher was ecstatic when his pone (pony) lost. Why?

Clues: 1. He had bet on the game. 2. His pone almost won.

Puzzle 3-50
It was approaching midnight when he began to prey (pray). With his head bent over, he was startled when something fell on him from behind. What happened?

Clues: 1. He was in a deep state of concentration. 2. At the moment, he thought he was alone.

Puzzle 3-51
The king's rein (reign) was coming to an end and he was terrified of dying. Why?

Clues: 1. He could see danger fast approaching. 2. He had no sons to carry on his name.

Puzzle 3-52
The weather was perfect on the ocean that day, but the sale (sail) didn't work as planned. What happened?

Clues: 1. They were on the boat and everything was in top condition. 2. They sailed for hours before coming to land.

Puzzle 3-53
He was getting exhausted, but when it was his turn to wrest (rest), he gathered his energy and moved ahead. Why?

Clues: 1. He wanted to finish. 2. Everyone had a chance to wrest.

Puzzle 3-54
The teacher was insistent that they were taut (taught) in the correct way. Why didn't anybody argue what the correct way was?

Clues: 1. He was speaking to the class. 2. They were focused on the task at hand.

Puzzle 3-55

She was in her flower garden planting new seeds. When she took time to smell the rows (rose), she gasped at the smell. Why?

Clues: 1. She was not gasping at a pleasurable smell. 2. Some of the plants were not large enough for blooms.

Puzzle 3-56

Everyone could clearly see who had administered the tocsin (toxin). Why?

Clues: 1. He wasn't trying to hide. 2. Nobody died as a result.

Puzzle 3-57

Timothy was turning ten and having a huge birthday party. He looked forward to his aunt's presence (presents) every year and couldn't wait to see what she got him. He opened up his gift, but was sorely disappointed. Why?

Clues: 1. He didn't get clothing. 2. The gift was perfect for a ten-year-old.

Puzzle 3-58

She doubted the ascent (assent) of the marital arrangement would go smoothly. Why?

Clues: 1. There was bad weather that day. 2. It was not a prearranged marriage.

Puzzle 3-59

The berth (birth) was very smooth, but the parents still did not sleep well. Why?

Clues: 1. Their children were not around. 2. They had a small area to sleep in.

Puzzle 3-60

The smaller, bolder (boulder) of the two made it more difficult for them to cross. Why?

Clues: 1. They were in a vehicle. 2. They were driving on a major interstate highway.

ⓔ *Alert!*

If you're solving these lateral thinking puzzles in a group setting, the puzzle-giver can opt to give the clues after a certain number of questions has been asked (determined ahead of time). When giving yes/no responses, she can also give a third answer of "irrelevant" if the group agrees to the rule.

Chapter 4
Wild Inventions

L ike all humans, you probably make mistakes here and there. Perhaps your mistakes occasionally turn out to be beneficial to you or others, however unintentional they were to begin with. Many inventions were created by accident, often while searching for the solution to a very different problem. The lateral thinking puzzles found in this chapter are mostly based on accidental inventions and the strange products that resulted. Other puzzles contain inventions that are interesting in their subject matter and their reason for development.

Puzzle 4-1
A doctor mixed a batch of medicine for his client and then drank it down himself. Why?

Clues: 1. It tasted good! 2. It worked better with a straw.

Puzzle: 4-2
The dentist saw something that gave him a way to terrify all of his patients. What was it?

Clues: 1. He didn't plan on using it himself. 2. Hopefully none of his patients would be subjected to it, either.

Puzzle 4-3
A woman opened up the grocery bag and even though she couldn't read, she knew that one of the items said "Wrigley's Gum." How?

Clues: 1. There was another identifiable part of the package. 2. Nobody told her what it was.

Puzzle 4-4
His snack was ruined, but others were willing to try it. What happened?

Clues: 1. It became a worldwide phenomena. 2. His snack was edible, just not in its original form.

Puzzle 4-5
If he had been more motivated he could have helped many people. How?

Clues: 1. He was a chemist. 2. He created something that he put aside as impractical.

Puzzle 4-6
The team won, and this product gained instant notoriety. What was it?

Clues: 1. It was a product designed specifically for that team. 2. It was not displayed or advertised during the game.

Puzzle 4-7
He spilled their breakfast and they cheered. Why?

Clues: 1. He did not spill it on the floor. 2. The meal was still edible.

Puzzle 4-8
He thought there had to be a better way to protect a table-cloth. His idea didn't work, but it helped in another way. What was it?

Clues: 1. His friend spilled wine on the tablecloth, staining it red. 2. The protection was meant to be clear to show the tablecloth's pattern and colors.

Puzzle 4-9
They were late returning to work and decided to try something new. It was delicious. What was it?

Clues: 1. They were late and their food was stale. 2. They worked in a health spa.

Puzzle 4-10
In the long term, the weaker one prevailed. Why?

Clues: 1. The inventor's intent was to create a stronger product. 2. The inventor ended up creating a weaker product that had better usage.

Puzzle 4-11
Their favorite food was considered sinful and was banned. What did they do to get around the prohibition?

Clues: 1. Teens loved this food in the late 1800s. 2. It's a sweet treat, still enjoyed today.

Puzzle 4-12
It was necessary for them to get messages across enemy lines. How did they do it?

Clues: 1. Nobody thought to suspect the innocent-looking object. 2. It took a lot of string.

Puzzle 4-13
They waited too long and missed the opportune time. They waited to see what would happen next and were pleased with the results. Why?

Clues: 1. It has to do with food. 2. They did not pick the crops in time.

Puzzle 4-14
It was beneficial to many that the goat herder was so observant. What did he see?

Clues: 1. He watched his goats exhibit some strange behavior. 2. He traced it back to the source and tried it himself.

Puzzle 4-15
The children continued to repeat history without even realizing it. Why?

Clues: 1. They were playing a game. 2. They knew nothing about the historical theme.

Puzzle 4-16
Lucky for the woman, her husband had access to his company's supplies. Why?

Clues: 1. She needed assistance. 2. He used some of the supplies to make her life simpler.

Puzzle 4-17

He desperately wanted to read more books, but nobody would help him. Why?

Clues: 1. He was able to read the books, but it took a good deal of time. 2. He only had access to a few books that he could read.

Puzzle 4-18

The accountant was playing around with different formulas when he stumbled on something new. What was it?

Clues: 1. He had a hobby that was quite different from his day job. 2. He loved keeping his mouth moving.

Puzzle 4-19

He didn't want to please the disgruntled guest, but for some reason his response was received favorably. What happened?

Clues: 1. The guest kept complaining so he purposely tried to annoy him. 2. The end product was a great treat.

Puzzle 4-20

The man was able to hear a sound that his neighbor could not. Minutes later his neighbor heard the sound, but he did not. What was going on?

Clues: 1. Only one person in the room at a time could hear the sound. 2. It was a pleasing sound.

Puzzle 4-21

His teaching tools sparked a wave of entertaining toys. What were they?

Clues: 1. He was teaching geography. 2. He was attempting to teach the various counties in his country.

Puzzle 4-22

It was a good thing for them that strawberry season didn't last all year. Why?

Clues: 1. The lack of strawberries forced them to think outside the box. 2. Their replacement was better accepted than the strawberries.

Fact

Merriam-Webster defines the word *invention* as a device, process, or discovery under U.S. patent law that is new and useful, that reflects extraordinary creative ability or skill, and that makes a distinct and recognized contribution to and advancement of science.

Puzzle 4-23

He was a hiker, and many of his ideas were inspired by nature. This invention was definitely one of them. What was it?

Clues: 1. He was hiking one day when it sprang to him. 2. He was annoyed at the inspiration.

Puzzle 4-24

His friend often needed help with menial tasks. He was a nice guy and tried to help. What did he do?

Clues: 1. His friend had a stiff back, which made it difficult to lean over. 2. His idea brought together two sides.

Puzzle 4-25

It was a cold day and Albert headed off to work. When he arrived he became frustrated, but he did something about it. What did he do?

Clues: 1. He was wearing his jacket to keep out the cold. 2. His work was heated and he no longer needed the jacket.

Puzzle 4-26

This product helped remove a family from slavery. What was it?

Clues: 1. The product was unrelated to slavery. 2. The man who invented the product helped the slaves.

Puzzle 4-27

He was treated with a reward for remembering his prayers. What was it?

Clues: 1. It was a twisted type of food. 2. It was a reward with dual meaning.

Puzzle 4-28

It was a great thing for him that mint juleps lose their flavor when they become warm. Why?

Clues: 1. He needed a new way to drink them. 2. He was an avid fan of the beverage.

Puzzle 4-29

They loved his samples, but didn't realize that they were supposed to remove the packaging first. What was it?

Clues: 1. It helped to quench their thirst. 2. The packaging didn't ruin the flavor and actually became a convenient way to handle the product.

Puzzle 4-30

Walter needed a way to pay off a $15 debt. He paid it off but could have made a much higher profit. What did he do?

Clues: 1. He had made many other inventions. 2. He was playing around with something from a workshop.

Puzzle 4-31

Kids loved that he was a naval engineer helping the war effort in 1943. Why?

Clues: 1. He accidentally knocked over something that gave him a great idea. 2. He was working to help stabilize ship equipment.

Puzzle 4-32

This tiny idea helped readers everywhere. How?

Clues: 1. It had nothing to do with helping the eyes. 2. The final result lessened the harshness of the written word.

Puzzle 4-33

If it weren't for him, it would be dangerous for tourists to see the New York skyline. Why?

Clues: 1. The answer is unrelated to products for the eyes. 2. There would be many steps to devise a work-around.

Puzzle 4-34

When she invented this product, it was initially mocked because people thought it would be too distracting. What was it?

Clues: 1. It was probably distracting at first, but proved very beneficial. 2. It was a turn-of-the-century (nineteenth to twentieth) invention.

Puzzle 4-35

She was adamant about wearing her slinky dress. Lucky for her friends and family, she wore it to an event. Why?

Clues: 1. Her dress was low-cut and sheer. 2. This was an early-twentieth-century invention.

Puzzle 4-36

She thought that housecleaning was a thankless, unending, boring job. So what did she do?

Clues: 1. She didn't hire a housecleaner. 2. She didn't move.

Puzzle 4-37

He was embarrassed about getting too close to a woman, so he created something. What was it?

Clues: 1. The women were his patients. 2. It was an early-nineteenth-century invention.

Puzzle 4-38

They discovered the easiest way to clean up after themselves. What was it?

Clues: 1. They didn't let somebody else clean for them. 2. It was a more recent invention.

Puzzle 4-39

Chocolate melted too easily, so this invention was created to help withstand the heat. What was it?

Clues: 1. It was a flavorful treat. 2. It did not help the melting chocolate.

 *Question?*

How do I solve these puzzles if I don't know much about inventions?
You don't need to be an invention buff to figure out the solutions to these puzzles. Inventors are always thinking outside the realm of existing products, and you'll need to do the same here. Put on your thinking cap and use the puzzles and the clues to figure out the appropriate inventions.

Puzzle 4-40
Originally a product targeted to adult smokers, it was later repackaged for children. What was it?

Clues: 1. It was not dangerous to children. 2. It was not candy cigarettes.

Puzzle 4-41
If at first you don't succeed, you should try another 39 times. Why?

Clues: 1. This product was perfected after 40 times. 2. Although not designed as a household product, it is now often seen in cupboards today.

Puzzle 4-42
Lucky for her employers, along with being an executive secretary who took pride in her work, she was also an artist. Why was it beneficial to them?

Clues: 1. She did not participate in any marketing for her employers. 2. She did not create an artistic display.

Puzzle 4-43
One day an idea for a new product fell in his lap. What was it?

Clues: 1. It did not fall from the sky. 2. It was not a pleasant experience.

Puzzle 4-44
He was just about to close a deal with an important client when a competing insurance broker stepped in and got the signed contract. What did he do?

Clues: 1. He had to step out for a moment, allowing the competing broker to step in. 2. He was determined never to allow it to happen again.

Puzzle 4-45
He hired models to use and demonstrate his product because men viewed it as effeminate, and young women viewed it as unstylish. What was it?

Clues: 1. It changed the way people shop. 2. He hated to see people struggle.

Puzzle 4-46
He got up one morning and decided to help his wife get the children ready for school. After making a complete mess of things, he thought he'd try something new. What was it?

Clues: 1. He was helping to make them breakfast. 2. They had to get their calcium.

Puzzle 4-47
His knowledge of fly-fishing worked to save many lives. What did he create?

Clues: 1. It was not a product for fishing. 2. He thought of a way to reel something out.

Puzzle 4-48
In 1562, Pope Gregory introduced a new calendar to the Christian world. Unfortunately, some citizens did not believe or hear about the changes. What happened?

Clues: 1. The previous calendar year started in the spring. 2. The new calendar year started on January 1st.

Puzzle 4-49

The desire to save time and a recent popular fascination combined perfectly for one man. What did he create?

Clues: 1. His creation also incorporated food and dinnertime. 2. He was hoping to find a use for holiday leftovers.

Puzzle 4-50

He never would have guessed that his product would be used in the office, home, for fun, and across most industries. What was it?

Clues: 1. It could be used as a standalone product. 2. It could be used as a coating.

Puzzle 4-51

The company began receiving complimentary letters, but the executives didn't know why the product was acting as it did. What happened?

Clues: 1. A mistake had occurred in the laboratory and was covered up. 2. They began making the product with the imperfection and still do today.

Puzzle 4-52

Sales of this product increased significantly after a life was saved. Why?

Clues: 1. It was a type of food. 2. Consumers saw that it was very effective.

Puzzle 4-53
His age and desire to read contributed to this invention. What was it?

Clues: 1. He could not see very well. 2. He hated switching out items.

Puzzle 4-54
A light-up flowerpot turned into a much bigger idea for one entrepreneur. What product did he invent?

Clues: 1. His new product had nothing to do with flowers or gardening. 2. He purchased the flowerpot at a low price from a friend.

Puzzle 4-55
He was fortunate that his neighbor was sick of soot being tracked around her house. What did he create?

Clues: 1. She used ashes in other locations besides her fireplace. 2. She loved the replacement for ashes and asked for more of the product.

Puzzle 4-56
They misunderstood the order for an earthenware jar and created a new product. What was it?

Clues: 1. The use of a particular word had decreased tremendously over the years. 2. The word sounded much like a modern word.

Puzzle 4-57

Originally a mistake, this product was marketed as a way to help prevent spreading colds among children. What was it?

Clues: 1. Children typically used toilet paper to wipe their runny noses. 2. This product replaced the toilet paper.

 Fact

Thomas Edison was a great inventor and speaker. Two of his famous quotes include: "Just because something doesn't do what you planned it to do doesn't mean it's useless," and "Results! Why man, I have gotten a lot of results. I know several thousand things that won't work."

Puzzle 4-58

A surplus of material led to this child's toy creation. When and what was it?

Clues: 1. The product was placed in a fun container and marketed specifically to children. 2. It was originally created for wartime uses.

Puzzle 4-59

The original prototype of this product required too much attention and too many adjustments. Although the second prototype was confusing, it allowed the user to work much faster and more efficiently. What was it?

Clues: 1. The system is still in use today, even though the underlying mechanisms are not. 2. In modern countries, the tool is used quite often.

Puzzle 4-60

The salesman told the vendor that his new product was fabulous. The phrase he used stuck, and the vendor trademarked it shortly thereafter. What is it?

Clues: 1. It was a slang phrase used in the late nineteenth century. 2. The product was later immortalized in a song.

Puzzle 4-61

It was a hot day in St. Louis when this new container was created. What was it?

Clues: 1. He quickly ran out of ways to serve his customers. 2. Luckily, his friend had an edible replacement.

Chapter 5
A Long Time Ago

Throughout history, people have performed interesting and perplexing tasks. Whether for monetary gain, personal success, cultural acceptance, or through accidental mishaps, the actions that they took part in affect your life today in many ways. Since many historical events resulted in bizarre behavior or activities, they lend themselves perfectly to lateral thinking puzzles. You'll have to stretch to place yourself in a variety of times, situations, and cultural differences to solve these puzzles.

Puzzle 5-1

A man opened his front door and was handed a business card from a used furniture dealer. He immediately drew his gun and threatened to shoot. Why?

Clues: 1. This happened in the early twentieth century. 2. Used furniture wasn't all he sold.

Puzzle 5-2

He saw his neighbors' faces and knew instantly that their cat had died. How?

Clues: 1. They were not crying. 2. They were not carrying the dead feline.

Puzzle 5-3

The masked man allowed himself to be recognized by the king. What happened after that?

Clues: 1. Many of his followers did the same. 2. He was wearing armor.

Puzzle 5-4

The boy went to bed and woke to find it was eleven days later. What happened?

Clues: 1. He was not in a coma. 2. He did not travel anywhere.

Puzzle 5-5
The man forgot to shave and was quickly stopped on the street. Why?

Clues: 1. He was not famous. 2. He had a full beard.

Puzzle 5-6
Charlotte's parents were surprised that she went to get tested for a disease since she had no symptoms and she had not been exposed. Why did Charlotte get the test?

Clues: 1. She was forced to get the test by law. 2. She tested negative.

Puzzle 5-7
The business owners wanted to increase and extend their sales after tourist season ended on Labor Day. What did they do?

Clues: 1. They did not have a sale on their merchandise. 2. They created an event to bring tourists.

Puzzle 5-8
The British Admiral wanted to watch a cricket match in which Britain was a participant. He took his fleet and they ported their ships. What happened?

Clues: 1. He ordered his fleet to accompany him. 2. He angered the Sultan of the country where the fleet ported.

Puzzle 5-9

The woman arose one morning and decided to shave her entire head. Why?

Clues: 1. She was not going through chemotherapy or radiation. 2. She thought it was beautiful.

Puzzle 5-10

Although she was very rarely angry, her servants were surprised when she smiled at them. Why?

Clues: 1. There was something different about the smile. 2. She started a new craze.

Puzzle 5-11

The man was able to eavesdrop on conversations and easily transport secret letters, without anyone suspecting that he was capable of such a task. How?

Clues: 1. He was easily disguised. 2. It was during the French Revolution.

Puzzle 5-12

His physicians and aides used a magnetometer to search for the bullet embedded in his body. Unfortunately, the results were inconclusive and they were unable to find the bullet. What happened?

Clues: 1. There was interference that they did not recognize. 2. The bullet was never found.

Essential

> Although solving puzzles based on historical events may seem like no fun at all, you just need to change your thoughts on the topic. Your goal isn't to study and memorize facts for a test; rather, it is to enjoy yourself and work your lateral thinking muscles to solve a riddle. If you learn an interesting tidbit, or discover a historical event that you refuse to be doomed to repeat, then that's an added perk!

Puzzle 5-13

The captain ordered blankets to be distributed to the enemies who were attacking the fort. He was not hoping to surrender, so why did he make the gesture?

Clues: 1. The enemies accepted the blankets. 2. The captain hoped they would use the blankets to keep warm.

Puzzle 5-14

He had no idea that coffee was so dangerous. What happened?

Clues: 1. He did not suffer from the coffee. 2. He died because he drank it.

Puzzle 5-15

Hiram Johnson wanted to be president, but turned down two different chances to become one. Why?

Clues: 1. He could not have predicted the future. 2. He was too proud to wait.

Puzzle 5-16

Although the man had not placed the humans in cages, he was not upset to see them there. Why?

Clues: 1. He was interested to see what they were doing. 2. He was not a physician or a psychiatrist.

Puzzle 5-17

He wanted to carry his wealth with him, but in a place that others could not steal it. What did he do?

Clues: 1. He did not keep it out of sight. 2. Others around him did the same with their wealth.

Puzzle 5-18

His neighbors thought he was possessed by the devil, causing him to be imprisoned for seven years. Explain.

Clues: 1. He was doing something that they had never seen before. 2. They were unwilling to try it.

Puzzle 5-19

He was wounded for life in order to protect her from committing an immoral act. He didn't even know her, so why did he do it?

Clues: 1. It was during the seventeenth and eighteenth centuries. 2. Many others had to undergo the procedure and often died from it.

Puzzle 5-20

Why did it cost over a thousand dollars to remove the lipstick?

Clues: 1. It left a stain. 2. The woman was unaware of the damage that would result from her kiss.

Puzzle 5-21

The spy brought back information about a planned sneak attack, but the colonel did nothing about it. Why?

Clues: 1. There's a good chance he never read the information. 2. The colonel was busy with other matters.

Puzzle 5-22

Hailed as the most powerful warship of its time, the boat quickly turned away before another ship could fire upon it. What happened?

Clues: 1. The captain was not a coward. 2. The boat was in friendly waters.

ⓔ Fact

"We can learn from history how past generations thought and acted, how they responded to the demands of their time, and how they solved their problems. We can learn by analogy, not by example, for our circumstances will always be different than theirs were." –Gerda Lerner

Puzzle 5-23

The craftsman washed the fabric, shaped it in a large cone, shrunk it in boiling water, and dried it. He then shaped it, smoothed it, and had his finished product. He then lurched out the door and incoherently tried to sell it. Explain.

Clues: 1. He was attempting to sell a hat. 2. Many of his colleagues acted the same way.

Puzzle 5-24

He was able to single-handedly capture a fully staffed fort during wartime. How did he do it?

Clues: 1. He had not planned on capturing the fort. 2. The enemies were attending a lecture.

Puzzle 5-25
The burglar was startled by the cops and quickly left the scene. He left only one, non-identifying thing behind and from that, the police were able to follow him home. What did he leave behind?

Clues: 1. He did not leave any footprints. 2. They did not follow his car.

Puzzle 5-26
The destroyer aimed at the target in the water during a live-fire exercise. The boat barely missed its mark, but the crew was abnormally upset. Why?

Clues: 1. They hit something else. 2. They were out of practice.

Puzzle 5-27
After poisoning sixteen people, twelve of whom died as a result, he was sentenced to death. His lawyers argued against the sentence and it was removed. Why?

Clues: 1. They were under military occupation. 2. Still today there is speculation that he did not commit the crime.

Puzzle 5-28
Even though they were about to be trapped by enemy forces, the army still refused to leave the area. Why?

Clues: 1. They were defeated as a result. 2. They were able to depart if they had chosen to.

Puzzle 5-29
He wanted to celebrate his election and inauguration with a great deal of fanfare and speeches. Unfortunately, it later caused his death. Why?

Clues: 1. It was the longest speech of its kind. 2. He underestimated the weather that day.

Puzzle 5-30
If they wanted to win, the contestants should have completed the marathon more slowly. Why?

Clues: 1. They did not follow the rules. 2. Their story was unconvincing.

Puzzle 5-31
Even though he was wounded, he refused to be treated. Why?

Clues: 1. He had access to a physician. 2. He did not believe that he was going to die.

Puzzle 5-32
He ran around naked in public, but nobody seemed to care. In fact, the majority of the others were naked as well. Why?

Clues: 1. He was not on a nude beach. 2. He was running a race.

Puzzle 5-33
His family sat around playing games when there was a knock on the door. He quickly picked up the dice and swallowed them. Why?

Clues: 1. He was paid to do so. 2. He was not taking a bribe.

Puzzle 5-34
He was working when he cut himself with a knife. Although the wound was a surface scratch, he later died as a result. What happened?

Clues: 1. He was not working with chemicals or metals. 2. He was infected from the scratch.

Puzzle 5-35
He only paid the doctor when he was not sick, and sometimes the doctor gave him money in return. Why?

Clues: 1. He was wealthy and was not on any sort of payment plan. 2. This was common practice.

Puzzle 5-36

For a several years, the teacher had to teach his students a different mnemonic device.

Clues: 1. The order of words changed, not just the words themselves. 2. Some teachers didn't bother teaching this part.

Puzzle 5-37

The restaurant owner threw out cases of unopened wine bottles at a huge loss to his revenue. Most of his customers would have drunk it, so why didn't he serve it?

Clues: 1. He drank a bottle of the wine. 2. He didn't want to risk the consequences.

Puzzle 5-38

He paused the game to try a new vegetable. He wasn't hungry, so why did he want it?

Clues: 1. He was not a chef. 2. He was playing in the game.

Puzzle 5-39

His boss told him to send his colleague a message, but instead he sent him a bunch of gibberish. Why?

Clues: 1. The words were understandable but they did not form coherent sentences. 2. The boss did not understand the message but the colleague did.

Puzzle 5-40
He could have sent any United States troops into battle without obtaining anyone's approval. How?

Clues: 1. He was not a military official. 2. He only had this power for a twenty-four-hour period.

Puzzle 5-41
He walked into a barbershop to get a shave, but came out bleeding. Why was the customer not upset with the barber for nicking him?

Clues: 1. The customer paid for the bleeding. 2. This occurred during the Middle Ages.

Puzzle 5-42
The army platoon was marching in step for a mile before purposely breaking step for the last fifty feet. Why were they not punished for not marching together?

Clues: 1. Their sergeant was around and also stepped out of the uniform march. 2. They were taking a precautionary measure.

Puzzle 5-43
Each day the postman brought him several tons of bricks in boxes. Why?

Clues: 1. He had ordered the bricks to be delivered. 2. The postman was not happy to have this current route.

Puzzle 5-44

He slipped and fell, causing his and his cousin's death. Another cousin was paralyzed from the accident. What happened?

Clues: 1. He did not fall on top of anything. 2. He fell from a great distance.

Puzzle 5-45

Betsy took her time picking out the perfect wallpaper for her mother-in-law. She picked a lovely rose shade for her bedroom, and a bright green tone for the kitchen. Years later Betsy's husband accused her of killing his mother. Why?

Clues: 1. He knew that she could not have done it on purpose. 2. She was devastated at the events that took place.

Puzzle 5-46

It was a clear winter evening, without a cloud in sight, but the airplane pilot chose to reroute his passengers slightly off course. Why?

Clues: 1. The pilot did this once a day for approximately three weeks, but he was not spying on anyone. 2. The passengers were different for each flight.

Puzzle 5-47
Why was he the first in his class to be able to write his middle name?

Clues: 1. He had a relatively easy name to write. 2. He often found it difficult to explain the meaning behind it.

Puzzle 5-48
The community did not like the surrounding neighborhoods, so many of the residents decided to move out of the state. Why didn't they pack any of their belongings?

Clues: 1. Their houses and belongings remained intact. 2. They did not have any reason to travel light.

Puzzle 5-49
He wanted to educate people about Christianity, but the church disagreed with his methods. He never deviated from what was in the Bible, so why did they condemn him and burn his body?

Clues: 1. He hoped to bring Christianity to many people. 2. He was brought to trial multiple times.

Puzzle 5-50
His rapid writing became an iconic way to look at things. Explain.

Clues: 1. His combination of letters created a symbol. 2. Over time the symbol took on a life of its own.

Puzzle 5-51

The feud between the two families lasted over seventeen years, and the mediators got their names on the map. Explain.

Clues: 1. This took place in the eighteenth century. 2. The families were not the Hatfields and the McCoys.

Alert!

The puzzles in this chapter date from the immediate past through ancient history. In working through your solution, try putting the information in different historical times. You might be better able to solve the puzzle when considering it in its correct setting.

Puzzle 5-52

The customer walked into the shop and handed the owner a piece of paper. The owner held it up to the light and then charged the customer accordingly. What was the shop owner looking at?

Clues: 1. The paper was not a receipt or bill. 2. The owner did not even read the writing.

Puzzle 5-53

The inhabitants were quite happy that a fire raged through the town, burning thousands of houses and injuring citizens. Over 400 acres were destroyed and several people died, so why were they pleased?

Clues: 1. They did not start the fire. 2. The fire prevented something worse from happening.

Puzzle 5-54

Jack was unemployed and broke, and one sunny day he was found walking aimlessly along the beach. A short time later he was worth over six million dollars. What happened?

Clues: 1. He did not think up a great idea. 2. He found something as he was walking.

Puzzle 5-55

He predicted his death would be related to his birth in a very specific way. What happened?

Clues: 1. There was a special event that occurred in conjunction with both his birth and death. 2. His prediction came true.

Puzzle 5-56

The first half of the book was edited multiple times as the years progressed, but the second half was left alone. Why?

Clues: 1. It was not the Bible. 2. The author was deceased when the alterations occurred.

Puzzle 5-57

The high-ranking advisor brought an extra 400 camels whenever he traveled. Why did they always walk in the same order?

Clues: 1. They did not carry people or food. 2. They were not killed or harmed in any way.

Puzzle 5-58

The queen had slaves that pampered her and attended to her every wish. Why did she outlaw slavery?

Clues: 1. She could afford to pay them. 2. Her history was not one typically related to royalty.

Puzzle 5-59

Up until the morning of the election, she was planning on voting for a particular candidate. That morning she changed her mind and decided to vote for herself. Why?

Clues: 1. She did not write her name on the list. 2. She won the election with a substantial amount of votes.

Puzzle 5-60

The man sat in the courtroom and assisted the prosecution by adding commentary to their side of the case. Why wasn't the defendant upset?

Clues: 1. The defendant was in the room. 2. The defendant had confessed to the murder.

Chapter 6
Around the World

Geography is a science that looks at both the features of the land and the effects of human activity on the land and the lives it touches. The puzzles contained in this chapter relate to various aspects of geography. You'll find puzzles that refer to bizarre landmarks or strange environmental occurrences. You'll also solve puzzles based on laws and situations that are unique to specific states and countries. It'll be a time for exploration and discovery as you learn about other cultures and regions around the globe.

Puzzle 6-1
A woman traveled to Bolivia on vacation. She arrived at her destination and immediately became sick. Why?

Clues: 1. She had bronchial problems. 2. She was expecting the illness.

Puzzle 6-2
He met a woman in Italy and immediately knew that she was not a prostitute. How?

Clues: 1. She was not a nun. 2. She did not tell him anything about her career.

Puzzle 6-3
The woman asked a nearby tourist to take a picture of her. She wanted to develop it and show her friends that she could be in four places at once. How?

Clues: 1. She did not turn back the clock on the camera. 2. Many people were doing the same thing.

Puzzle 6-4
What is the fewest number of states (in the United States) you could travel through if you drove for 2,000 miles without stopping?

Clues: 1. It doesn't matter where you start. 2. You don't need a map to figure it out.

Puzzle 6-5
Assuming that you had to travel at least one mile into each state, what is the largest number of state borders (in the United States) you could cross while driving 500 miles continuously?

Clues: 1. You don't need a map to figure it out. 2. It doesn't matter where you start.

Puzzle 6-6
He traveled for miles and miles, and although he didn't see a river, or any other significant landmarks, he knew exactly where he was. How?

Clues: 1. He was alone and did not have a map. 2. He did not have a compass.

Puzzle 6-7
She purchased land in her country of origin, but hired an architect in New York. He designed the estate of her dreams in his state, but when she went back home to build it, major changes had to occur. Why?

Clues: 1. The architect had seen the land and there were no structural issues. 2. The architect had been unaware of a particular law.

Puzzle 6-8

A man casually walked through the park, taking pictures of people as they strolled through on their lunch hour. Why?

Clues: 1. He was hoping to make a profit. 2. He was not looking to take a picture of a specific person.

Puzzle 6-9

He was visiting Japan and borrowed his friend's car. When he saw the light turn green, he drove forward and caused an accident. What happened?

Clues: 1. He made a bad assumption. 2. He drove the car properly.

Puzzle 6-10

She told him that she had him in the palm of her hand. Why?

Clues: 1. She loved him very much. 2. She was trying to make a point.

Puzzle 6-11

She would rather have gone to the hospital after jumping off the bridge. Why?

Clues: 1. She jumped on purpose. 2. She didn't know the ramifications of her actions.

Puzzle 6-12

Manuela lived in Mexico and wanted to come to the United States. She crossed the border, illegally, right in front of the border patrol. They saw her and arrested her. She was not unhappy that this occurred. Why?

Clues: 1. She was not afraid of being sent back to Mexico. 2. She was not in any danger.

Puzzle 6-13

Although her husband didn't help much with the housework or raising the children, he made sure to do one task for her each morning before going to work. What was it?

Clues: 1. She did not need to remind him to do it. 2. It's the same task every day.

Puzzle 6-14

The family took a burnt baby doll to the hospital. Why?

Clues: 1. They did not know it was a doll. 2. They were concerned about the doll's heritage.

Puzzle 6-15

It was rainy and warm, so a Delaware road was closed to traffic for several days. There was no flooding, so why did it close?

Clues: 1. There was nothing blocking the street. 2. The road was in a park.

Puzzle 6-16
A married couple was ordered to regard each other as brother and sister. Why?

Clues: 1. They were not related by birth. 2. Their marriage was viewed as sinful.

Puzzle 6-17
Ralph was driving along the highway when he pulled into the left lane to pass a car. He was pulled over a few minutes later. Why?

Clues: 1. He was not speeding. 2. His brake lights were working and his registration was current.

Puzzle 6-18
Years later, the boy was glad the government stepped in against his father on his behalf. The boy wasn't being abused, so why did the government intervene?

Clues: 1. The father was attempting to break the law. 2. The son was in no danger.

Puzzle 6-19
The couple wanted to visit a royal palace on their honeymoon. They were United States citizens and did not have passports, so what did they do?

Clues: 1. They were able to get their wish. 2. They stayed within the United States.

Puzzle 6-20

They were riding in a boat, and although there was no funeral, every vessel they passed was painted black. Why?

Clues: 1. They were on a romantic boat tour. 2. They were visiting a city in Europe.

 *Question?*

Where did these strange facts come from?
The puzzles in this book are based on geography and cultural facts that were gathered through books, magazines, and Internet pages. Each time the information was garnered, the facts were double-checked against other sources to determine their authenticity.

Puzzle 6-21

While only walking in a small radius, she was able to see five states in ten minutes. How?

Clues: 1. She was not looking through a telescope. 2. She was not in an airplane or space shuttle.

Puzzle 6-22

He was talking to his friend when he was pulled over by a policeman. Why?

Clues: 1. He was driving a car. 2. His friend was not in the car.

Puzzle 6-23

Even though her husband was jailed for beating her, the woman was denied a divorce. Why?

Clues: 1. Her husband was not protesting the divorce. 2. The divorce was from her current husband.

Puzzle 6-24

He was lucky it was a warm day because nobody noticed the weapon that he openly carried. Why?

Clues: 1. He would not have hidden the weapon if he wore more clothing. 2. He needed something to cool him off.

Puzzle 6-25

Kerri came back from summer vacation and spoke of her adventures to her classmates. At one point she told them that she had seen a sunrise on the Pacific Ocean and saw the sunset on the Atlantic Ocean. She burst into tears when her classmate called her a liar. Was she telling the truth?

Clues: 1. She had seen the two events on the same day. 2. She had traveled outside of the United States.

Puzzle 6-26
The caravan was traveling across the desert. They brought no water for their horses, and they did not meet up with anyone else along their trip. How did the horses survive?

Clues: 1. The horses were not carried across the desert. 2. They discovered a way to get water as they traveled.

Puzzle 6-27
Residents of Calcutta recently married two decorated trees to one another in an elaborate ceremony. Why?

Clues: 1. The trees were considered sacred. 2. Many people attended the ceremony.

Puzzle 6-28
Why did the man jump over multiple babies?

Clues: 1. The mothers were not concerned. 2. The men rarely missed.

Puzzle 6-29
The pilot landed the airplane in the middle of a cloud. How?

Clues: 1. The cloud was on the ground. 2. The airplane had no special equipment.

Puzzle 6-30
Tom was given a ticket for eating a bag of potato chips in his vehicle. Why?

Clues: 1. He was driving the car. 2. A police officer wrote Tom a ticket.

Puzzle 6-31
Why did the family willingly eat rust with their food?

Clues: 1. They knew that the rust was there. 2. They believed there were no safety concerns.

Puzzle 6-32
He purposely asked the doctor to allow the wound to heal badly. The doctor could have competently stitched it up, so why did the patient want a scar?

Clues: 1. He was not afraid of the doctor's handiwork. 2. He wanted to show off his wounds.

Puzzle 6-33
They called a news station with information on a whale sighting in the desert. Explain.

Clues: 1. They were of sound mental health. 2. They had uncovered something phenomenal.

Fact

Although knowledge of geography and cultures will be of some assistance when solving these puzzles, they are not a necessity. If you don't know much about other states, countries, or planets, just use the lateral thinking process to tackle the puzzle. Ask inventive questions and try to narrow down the possible solutions.

Puzzle 6-34

While playing off the twelfth hole, a golfer hit the ball and watched it land. He decided to tee off again, but was not penalized a stroke by the other members in his foursome. Why?

Clues: 1. He had access to his first ball, but decided to leave it be. 2. The players waited a few minutes to see whether the ball would move.

Puzzle 6-35

The women bought many condoms even though they had no plans to use them for sexual purposes. Explain.

Clues: 1. They were not giving the condoms away to others. 2. They used the condoms for their craft.

Puzzle 6-36

Erin had recently taken a cruise to Hawaii, the most southern state in the United States, and wanted to see the remaining directional extremes. She decided to try to see the most northern, most eastern, and most western states, all in the same day. Erin was petrified of flying, so how could she make her dream come true?

Clues: 1. She did not view pictures or videos of the states. 2. She did not travel very far.

Puzzle 6-37

The tourist walked into a store and purchased some traditional items to take back home as gifts. The shop owner gave him his change and the tourist immediately knew he was being swindled. How?

Clues: 1. The tourist did not have to count the money. 2. The shop owner relented and gave him the correct amount.

Puzzle 6-38

After a lengthy discussion between the two neighbors, one man held out an onion to the other. When his neighbor refused to take it, the first man became enraged and called the other a liar. Why?

Clues: 1. It had to do with the onion. 2. They had come to an agreement and needed to seal the deal.

Puzzle 6-39

The tourist lost his bags during his trip and had to purchase new toiletries when he arrived at the hotel. He was able to purchase toothpaste and mouthwash, but had to improvise when it came to using a toothbrush. Why?

Clues: 1. He arrived on a Sunday. 2. The store was extremely cautious.

Puzzle 6-40

George peeked out from under the cover of the Thanksgiving Day float he was riding on. He grabbed his pistol and shot a nearby man on a horse that was also in the parade. The man was wounded and sent to the hospital. Why was George not charged with any crime?

Clues: 1. The man wanted to press charges. 2. George knew he would not be charged before attempting the shot.

Puzzle 6-41

Although the best friends usually exchanged hugs, that day they just knocked their knees against one another. As they looked around the room, they noticed many others were doing the same. Why?

Clues: 1. It was not a type of dance. 2. The friends were worried.

Puzzle 6-42

She had her own servants, guards, and private palace, even though she was not related to the royal family. How?

Clues: 1. This occurred in China. 2. She was considered royalty.

Essential

Many states and countries around the world have outdated laws or downright bizarre legislation. A few of these puzzles are based on these odd facts, giving you a chance to learn more about odd illegal actions and strange government rulings. Just don't take a bath more than once a week in Massachusetts; it's against the law.

Puzzle 6-43

Even though they were not traveling outside the United States, they had to learn to drive on the left side of the road. Why?

Clues: 1. Traffic congestion was a concern. 2. The idea was based on a European intersection.

Puzzle 6-44

They placed the flag in a place where it could fly all day and night, would not be raised or lowered, and could not easily be saluted. Where is it?

Clues: 1. Nobody has touched it in over three decades. 2. It is not visible with the naked eye.

Puzzle 6-45
Samuel stood on the ground looking up at a 50-foot tall cliff. He needed to reach the top, where his car was parked, but there was no way for him to scale the almost vertical wall of earth. Samuel did not have any rock-climbing equipment, so what did he do?

Clues: 1. Samuel was on the beach. 2. He waited about six hours to reach the top.

Puzzle 6-46
Where does one tenth of the world population live?

Clues: 1. You're not looking for a specific country or continent. 2. Think smaller.

Puzzle 6-47
Where do approximately 50 percent of Americans live?

Clues: 1. Not in one particular state. 2. Not within a time zone.

Puzzle 6-48
Jennifer was looking to get a condominium with a view of the water. Her real estate agent said she could get her a place right on the bay, but Jennifer declined the offer. Why?

Clues: 1. She wanted to move in quickly. 2. She wasn't sure if the view would be of any water.

Puzzle 6-49
They went to visit Santa Claus in the middle of summer. They did not travel to the North Pole, so how is this possible?

Clues: 1. They did not sit on his lap. 2. They did not know anyone named Santa Claus.

Puzzle 6-50
Craig stood in line and ordered a sandwich for lunch. As he moved to the side to wait for his meal, the gentleman behind him ordered his meal. How did Craig know that the man was a tourist?

Clues: 1. He did not have an accent. 2. He ordered something particular from the menu.

Puzzle 6-51
Katherine drove into the state and knew exactly where to go to find tourist information. She did not see any signs with the location, nor did anyone tell her where to go. How did she know?

Clues: 1. She could tell from looking at other cars. 2. She was able to quickly pull up information.

Puzzle 6-52

She lived within the border of the United States, but did not live in a state. She did not live in Washington D.C., so where did she reside?

Clues: 1. She could have lived in more than one location. 2. Others around her did not live in a state as well.

Puzzle 6-53

Shirley's dog began barking at night and her cat hid under the bed. She decided to drive to her parents' house the next day and brought her animals with her. Why?

Clues: 1. She did not leave the animals at her parents' home. 2. They had exhibited this behavior in the past.

Puzzle 6-54

John was traveling to see his brother. His brother gave him specific directions to the hotel where he was staying in the capital city. Why did John call his brother, upset because he was unable to locate the address?

Clues: 1. John took a taxi and the driver had never heard of the hotel. 2. John was in the correct country.

Puzzle 6-55

The doctor was surprised to learn that the temperature never got above 40 degrees Fahrenheit, even though she was in the desert. Explain.

Clues: 1. She knew the temperature would be chilly. 2. The location rarely received any rain.

Puzzle 6-56

It was 1:00 in the morning when Jennifer woke up to the sound of a jackhammer. For the third night in a row, she peeked out her blinds and saw construction work being completed on the road below. The men were not using any lights, so how were they able to work?

Clues: 1. It was a new moon. 2. This occurred during a specific time of year.

Puzzle 6-57

The little boy wanted to find out more about his new pet frog. He searched through books and found that the amphibian was native to North Africa. He was startled to see this, considering he lived in Greece. Explain.

Clues: 1. He was not sent the frog from a friend, nor did he purchase it from a catalog or the Internet. 2. The frogs appeared in his yard one cloudy afternoon.

Puzzle 6-58

For four months out of the year, any mail addressed to the hotel is sent directly to the hotel lobby. The remaining eight months of the year packages are sent to a post office box. Why?

Clues: 1. The time of year is important. 2. The hotel is not available for a portion of the year.

Puzzle 6-59

Jeanette lay out in the sun, clad only in her bathing suit. She relaxed, reading a book for hours, without applying any sunscreen. Why did she not experience any sunburn?

Clues: 1. Jeanette had pale skin. 2. She knew ahead of time that she would not need to wear sunscreen.

Chapter 7
Urban Legends

Urban legends are tales and stories that can be funny or horrifying, true or false. They spread quickly through word of mouth, letters, and more recently through e-mail and the Internet. Because of the bizarre nature and twists involved in urban legends, they easily convert to lateral thinking puzzles. This chapter contains puzzles all based on urban legends, whether they are true, false, or unconfirmed.

Puzzle 7-1

A young man stopped by a local convenience store to purchase a 16-ounce soda. He guzzled it down and quickly drove home. Why?

Clues: 1. What he drank is important. 2. He was hoping his girlfriend would be alone.

Puzzle 7-2

She saw the lights, rifled through her purse to find a penny, and popped it in her mouth. Why?

Clues: 1. The lights were from an approaching car. 2. She was hoping the penny would assist her.

Puzzle 7-3

A man got into an argument with his wife. After she went to bed, he decided to get some fresh air and have a few beers. After his fourth beer he had to use the restroom, ultimately causing his death. How?

Clues: 1. He did not move much to go to the bathroom. 2. Drinking alcohol had little to do with his death.

Puzzle 7-4

The man was buried in a concrete structure above ground. Why?

Clues: 1. His wife was paid a good amount of money. 2. The company he worked for was cost conscious.

Puzzle 7-5

The woman arrived home and ran in to pick up the phone that was ringing. It was her veterinarian. He told her to leave the house immediately and to call the police. Why?

Clues: 1. Her dog was choking when she found him and took him to the veterinarian. 2. The veterinarian was anxious about what she found in the dog's throat.

Puzzle 7-6

The thief stood outside the bank for hours, taking customers' money without using a gun or threats. How?

Clues: 1. He had a calm demeanor. 2. He looked very honest.

Fact

Some urban legends have existed for hundreds of years, changing only slightly as the story is told countless times. Others were created to reflect modern circumstances and conveniences. The name "urban legend" is intended to differentiate the tales from traditional folklore.

Puzzle 7-7

A woman was contemplating suicide when her phone rang. Five minutes later, she decided not to take her life. Why?

Clues: 1. She did not pick up the phone. 2. Something about the ring changed her mind.

Puzzle 7-8
The bus driver picked up twenty people at a bus stop. He then took them to a nearby insane asylum and dropped them off. Why?

Clues: 1. He worked for the insane asylum frequently. 2. He made an unusual stop on this trip.

Puzzle 7-9
She picked up the phone, had a heart attack, and died. What happened?

Clues: 1. She wasn't expecting a phone call from this person. 2. It startled her and she had the heart attack.

Puzzle 7-10
A woman was out in the woods with her boyfriend when he decided to go to the bathroom. She became scared and drove off, causing his death. Why?

Clues: 1. She did not back over him. 2. She did not leave him to die.

Puzzle 7-11
Although he attempted suicide by jumping out of a window, he actually killed himself with a gunshot. How?

Clues: 1. He landed in a safety net, which would have saved him from death. 2. He wasn't being shot on purpose.

Essential

> Urban legends are often told as cautionary tales or moral stories. The reader is warned of a possible situation, with just enough horror to make him take notice. He is then more likely to forward this information to family and friends so that they become knowledgeable on the subject as well. The urban legend continues to be passed along until somebody disputes the fact.

Puzzle 7-12

The thief opened the bag she had just stolen, gasped, and fell to the floor. Why?

Clues: 1. She was expecting to find a recent purchase. 2. She took the bag off the roof of a car in the parking lot.

Puzzle 7-13

Katherine snuck into her dorm room to find her toothbrush and a change of clothes before going back to her boyfriend's apartment. She did something that ultimately saved her life. What was it?

Clues: 1. She didn't want to disturb her roommate. 2. She was quiet, but not quiet enough.

Puzzle 7-14

NASA had created a gun that launched dead chickens at the windshields of airplanes and the space shuttle, to simulate collisions with airborne fowl. The test was designed to determine if the windshields were strong enough. British engineers learned of the gun and wanted to test it on their new high-speed train. Unfortunately, the chicken shattered the windshield, smashed the controls, and broke the engineer's chair. The engineers were horrified and sent the results to NASA. The engineers received a very short reply. What did it say?

Clues: 1. The engineers forgot an important step. 2. The engineers were embarrassed.

Puzzle 7-15

The woman pushed her beloved pet dog off her lap and began to scream. Why?

Clues: 1. He had not bitten her. 2. They were in a foreign country.

Puzzle 7-16

The gas station attendant lied and yelled out to her that she hadn't paid for the gas. Why?

Clues: 1. She had already left the building. 2. He wanted to see her again.

Puzzle 7-17

George was baffled when he arrived home and found his son's pet rabbit in its cage outside. Why?

Clues: 1. The rabbit had started off outside. 2. The rabbit did not belong in the cage.

Puzzle 7-18

He walked through the living room where his wife lay dead, and headed to the kitchen for some coffee. Why?

Clues: 1. He saw his wife lying there. 2. He did not kill her.

Puzzle 7-19

The group of Egyptians uncovered a bottle of honey near the Pyramids and began to eat it. They all quickly became sick. Why?

Clues: 1. The honey was not poisonous. 2. The honey was perfectly preserved.

Puzzle 7-20

They opened up the package to find a jar of grey powder. The children mixed it with some water and tried the new drink mix. It didn't taste that great and they were shocked to find out why.

Clues: 1. The powder wasn't meant to be mixed with water. 2. They were disgusted when they discovered what the powder was, weeks later.

Puzzle 7-21
She took a bath, and subsequently died hours later. What happened?

Clues: 1. She did not drown. 2. She was attempting to be fashionable.

Puzzle 7-22
The parents called the babysitter in the middle of the event to check in. She said that everything was going great and the food was in the oven. The parents immediately rushed home. Why?

Clues: 1. The babysitter thought the parents would be hungry when they returned home. 2. The parents were alarmed after the phone call.

Puzzle 7-23
The golfer became very impatient with his friends and hurried on to the next hole. Hours later they couldn't find him and he turned up dead after a few days. How did he die?

Clues: 1. He was playing in Palm Beach, Florida. 2. He did not commit suicide.

Puzzle 7-24

The two men were not pleased after they participated in the tug-of-war contest. What happened?

Clues: 1. This true event took place in Japan in 1997. 2. The two men were not on the same side.

Puzzle 7-25

His part time job at the Halloween Haunted House cost him his life. How?

Clues: 1. It was part of his routine. 2. It was an accidental suicide.

Puzzle 7-26

Living near the lake cost him his daughters' lives. How?

Clues: 1. Many other people died. 2. The lake was the cause.

Puzzle 7-27

He lay dead on the floor, cell phone in hand. What happened?

Clues: 1. He was not calling for help. 2. His death was accidental.

Puzzle 7-28

Josh was golfing one afternoon. He walked up to each hole, took the tee out of his mouth, and hit the ball. Two days later he died.

Clues: 1. He did not choke on the tee. 2. It was an accidental death.

Puzzle 7-29

She saw the elevator operator's face; it saved her life. Why?

Clues: 1. She did not know the operator, but had seen his face before. 2. The operator was alive.

Puzzle 7-30

A mother and daughter checked into separate rooms of a hotel due to the heavy volume of people coming in for the 1889 Paris Great Exposition. The mother was sick and the daughter went to find a doctor. The doctor said she was seriously ill and sent the daughter to his office to get some medicine. It took hours for the daughter to travel across town and back. She arrived back at the hotel and her mother was gone. There was no mention of her on the roster, and the room where she was staying had completely different furnishings and wallpaper. The daughter questioned the managers, doctors, and staff but her questioning seemed to confuse everyone. What happened?

Clues: 1. The daughter slowly went crazy as she continued the search for her mother. 2. She was at the correct hotel.

Puzzle 7-31
She stuck her head in the oven, turned on the gas, and waited to die. Hours later she was still alive. What happened?

Clues: 1. She turned the dial correctly. 2. She was alone in the house so nobody could pull her out.

Puzzle 7-32
The parents went away on vacation and came home to find their baby dead. How did it happen?

Clues: 1. They had hired a babysitter for the week they would be gone. 2. The baby was alive when they left.

Puzzle 7-33
She pulled out the nail with a hammer and ten minutes later there was a knock on the door. Why?

Clues: 1. She was told never to touch the nail. 2. The nail served a purpose.

Puzzle 7-34
A convict, in prison for committing armed robbery, sent a letter to his wife disclosing the location of some money and drugs. He knew that a prison employee would read the letter before sending it, so why did he write it down?

Clues: 1. He sent it on purpose. 2. He was hoping the police would react to the letter.

Puzzle 7-35
He purchased the picture because he liked the frame, but he got much more than he intended. Why?

Clues: 1. He was pleasantly surprised. 2. He had to take apart the frame.

Puzzle 7-36
He read the newspaper and shot himself in the head. Why?

Clues: 1. He was specifically checking for information. 2. He was distraught over something that he had not done.

Puzzle 7-37
Six months after a trip to Hawaii, the couple sent a note to the hotel they had vacationed in. Why?

Clues: 1. They attached a package with the note. 2. They had contemplated flying to Hawaii themselves.

Puzzle 7-38
Instead of buying in bulk and saving money, he bought hundreds of individual servings of pudding. Why?

Clues: 1. He did not own a restaurant. 2. He did not plan on eating all of the pudding.

Fact

> Urban legends are usually told through a narrator as happening to a "friend of a friend" so that the story has some credibility. If you believe your friend, and you assume that she believes her friend, you are more likely to believe the tale yourself.

Puzzle 7-39

She committed the first bridge murder. What happened?

Clues: 1. She murdered her husband. 2. She was angry over something they did quite often.

Puzzle 7-40

Carrie's car was hijacked without the use of weapons or threats. How?

Clues: 1. She thought she could trust the hijacker. 2. She woke up later with a headache.

Puzzle 7-41

It was unfortunate that Joseph stopped at that particular ATM machine that night. Why?

Clues: 1. He got off work and decided to deposit his tips. 2. He met nobody at the ATM.

Puzzle 7-42

The boy threw away his dead father's boots, even though it was all he had to remember him by. Why?

Clues: 1. They would have fit him. 2. He loved his father.

Puzzle 7-43

On every shift that he worked, Carter stole something from the company he worked for. He walked past the security guard, who checked everything thoroughly, and was never caught. How?

Clues: 1. He was not hiding the object he stole. 2. The security guard suspected that something was going on.

Puzzle 7-44

Because she sneaked out of the house to go to a party, her parents died.

Clues: 1. They discovered she had left. 2. She was being careless.

Puzzle 7-45

He never should have asked his wife to sell his luxury car. Why?

Clues: 1. She was extremely upset. 2. She didn't care who bought the car.

Puzzle 7-46
The students should have gotten their story straight. The teacher could tell they were lying. How?

Clues: 1. They made up a story to tell their teacher. 2. They didn't straighten out all the facts.

Puzzle 7-47
The teacher knew his student had plagiarized the assignment, but he gave him an A regardless. Why?

Clues: 1. It was a well-written paper. 2. The student was in college.

Puzzle 7-48
Five young girls were having a slumber party and began to tell ghost stories late one night. One of the girls said that a man had been buried alive earlier in the week, and if you went to the graveyard you could hear him scratching on the top of the coffin. Her friends called her bluff and said she was too afraid to go visit the graveyard. She took the challenge, but shouldn't have. Why?

Clues: 1. The man was, in fact, dead. 2. She saw nobody else in the graveyard.

Puzzle 7-49
Janet was running behind and was late getting ready for a date with her new boyfriend. Unfortunately, she didn't think things through and died as a result. Why?

Clues: 1. Her hair was still wet from her shower. 2. She thought she could speed things along.

Puzzle 7-50
A woman was standing on her front porch when she felt a sharp pain in her lower abdomen and began bleeding through her dress. The doctors retrieved a bullet, apparently shot from over 100 feet away. Later that year her husband requested a divorce. Why?

Clues: 1. He had reason to believe she was having an affair. 2. The gunshot was unintentional.

Puzzle 7-51
After trying unsuccessfully to unclog his toilets, the man called a plumber to come fix the problem. His wife was not happy when she arrived home.

Clues: 1. The plumber discovered something. 2. The man was not very pleased and confronted his wife.

Puzzle 7-52
After being lied to in previous relationships, Katherine came up with a way to tell if her new boyfriend was married or involved with another woman. How?

Clues: 1. She didn't spy on him. 2. He willingly provided the answer.

Puzzle 7-53
Laura answered the phone and was asked to take a survey. She hung up and called her husband, asking him to tell her the truth. What did he say?

Clues: 1. The company asked for a specific name. 2. Laura wished she could have taken the survey.

Puzzle 7-54
Anne was at a slumber party with her best friends. Before going to bed she went into the bathroom. A few minutes later she came out, pale as a ghost. Why?

Clues: 1. She did not have to go to the bathroom. 2. She did not see anything that would frighten her.

Puzzle 7-55
Martha made banana bread for all of her friends. The next day she asked for all but one of the loaves back. Why?

Clues: 1. She read something that frightened her. 2. She didn't want to harm her friends.

Puzzle 7-56

The mother knew that fast food wasn't good for her toddler, but she never thought that it would kill him. What happened?

Clues: 1. He did not develop heart disease. 2. He died from a trip to the fast food restaurant.

Puzzle 7-57

He knew within the course of thirty seconds that the stranger sitting next to him had had a stroke. How?

Clues: 1. There were certain questions to ask. 2. The man could not follow the directions correctly.

Puzzle 7-58

Although he knew roulette was a game of chance, he was able to win quite a lot of money. How?

Clues: 1. He won at one specific casino. 2. He performed a good deal of research.

Chapter 8
Occupational Hazards

Most people work a minimum of eight hours a day, five days a week. So, strange events are bound to occur during all that time you spend at work, right? And surely you've had odd jobs along your career path. Those bizarre work circumstances relate perfectly to lateral thinking puzzles, and should be an interesting topic in which you'll search for solutions. Draw on your own experience, and think creatively to solve these.

Puzzle 8-1
The engineers calculated the weight of the building and the architects designed a structure to support it. Yet every year it sinks further into the ground. Why?

Clues: 1. They didn't think of everything. 2. The architects weren't to blame.

Puzzle 8-2
The lights went dim, and then the room went dark. The man knew that he had lost his job. Why?

Clues: 1. The light was old. 2. He was asleep at the time.

Puzzle 8-3
The owner of a bedding store was very upset when his latest supply of pillows arrived from the manufacturer. When he complained to the manufacturer, what was he told?

Clues: 1. The owner was not pleased with the response. 2. He was hoping for the same service as previous orders.

Puzzle 8-4
The manager recorded the entire conversation he had with his employee without using a tape. How?

Clues: 1. He did not use a voice recorder. 2. He did not have someone else record it for him.

Puzzle 8-5
He left his hometown at 8:00 a.m. and arrived at work at 6:00 a.m. the same day. How?

Clues: 1. He lived in a different country from his office. 2. He was traveling quite rapidly.

Puzzle 8-6
When Diane's date arrived, she could tell that he was an attorney before he said a word.

Clues: 1. He did not hand her a business card. 2. He did not have any article of clothing or a briefcase that was monogrammed.

Puzzle 8-7
Kendra was not upset when her boss came up to touch her. Why?

Clues: 1. They were not romantically involved. 2. He was not shaking her hand.

Puzzle 8-8
The police officer walked up to his colleague's house to investigate a noise. He saw someone moving inside, but did not stop the thief. What happened?

Clues: 1. He was not harmed. 2. He was embarrassed.

Puzzle 8-9

She was glad she pulled over when the police signaled her to stop. Why?

Clues: 1. She thought she was speeding and was afraid to get a ticket. 2. She was not in any danger.

Puzzle 8-10

It was a good thing that Trent had enough fuel in his vehicle. Why?

Clues: 1. He kept signaling for assistance. 2. His vehicle was in perfect working order.

 Essential

As the times change, so do the job titles. With the advent of the Internet industry, many new job descriptions and job titles came into being. It has become quite a trend to have a lengthy, obscure title on your business card. One school in Scottsdale, Arizona, changed their receptionist to a "Director of First Impressions." Not so bad, is it?

Puzzle 8-11

Cindy should not have been so anxious about going to college. Why?

Clues: 1. She should have waited like the remaining applicants. 2. She should not have taken a shortcut.

Puzzle 8-12
They made their decision and he retired the next day, ending his career in that field. Why?

Clues: 1. He wasn't surprised at the decision. 2. He knew that he was no longer respected.

Puzzle 8-13
He was fired from his job after he notified residents of a local natural disaster. Why?

Clues: 1. The natural disaster had not occurred. 2. He was attempting to help the citizens.

Puzzle 8-14
The prosecutor ordered Carter Jones to court for a pretrial hearing in a murder case. When he arrived, the deputy would not let him in. Why?

Clues: 1. Carter had been subpoenaed and arrived on time. 2. He was not in any trouble and was later dismissed from the witness list.

Puzzle 8-15
Without using any equipment, how was a group of scientists able to conclude that a submarine used a loud burst of sonar during a training exercise?

Clues: 1. They did not know it was going to occur. 2. They never received proof from the government.

Puzzle 8-16

The burglar attempted to rob a convenience store, but left angry when the clerk began to laugh at him. What happened?

Clues: 1. The clerk did not mean to provoke him. 2. He was not telling any jokes.

Puzzle 8-17

Catherine awoke to find herself on a gurney in the morgue. What happened?

Clues: 1. She did not suffer a heart attack. 2. She did not come from a hospital.

Puzzle 8-18

The nurse came out to the waiting room. She told the patient "the doctor is in, but he can't see you now." Why?

Clues: 1. The patient was not upset. 2. The patient did not have to wait to be seen.

Puzzle 8-19

Why did the employee agree to take a drastic salary cut?

Clues: 1. He was not demoted. 2. He chose to take the cut, rather than the proposed increase.

Puzzle 8-20

The thief entered the store carrying a gun and a pillow-case over his head to disguise his appearance. After he threatened the cashier and received the money, a customer recognized him as he left the building. How?

Clues: 1. He did not have any distinguishing marks or tattoos. 2. The customer did not recognize his voice.

Puzzle 8-21

The armored truck guard was killed one morning as he and the driver of the truck transported money to and from various businesses. There was no car accident or any incident involving the truck being burglarized. What happened?

Clues: 1. The death was accidental. 2. The truck was badly designed.

 Alert!

In many of these puzzles, the occupation of the person in the situation is that of a thief, robber, or criminal. The activity is certainly not being condoned in this book, rather it is used in these lateral thinking puzzles because many thieves find themselves in crimes that have gone wrong.

Puzzle 8-22
The librarian charged the student a fine for returning the reference books late. The librarian then turned around and paid the fee himself. Why?

Clues: 1. He did not feel bad for the child. 2. He knew that the fine would not get paid otherwise.

Puzzle 8-23
Ralph traveled often on business trips. Depending on where he was flying, he used one of two preferred airline companies. When he flew with one company, he never had problems with his checked baggage. When Ralph flew with the other company, his luggage was often lost and it took at least one day to receive it. Explain.

Clues: 1. He always checked at least one bag, with either of the airlines. 2. Ralph was unaware of what other customers were doing around him.

Puzzle 8-24
The woman wanted to protest against an event that she viewed as a barbaric hunting of animals. She did not venture anywhere near the location of the hunt, so what did she do?

Clues: 1. She detailed the hunt to others. 2. She lost her job as a result.

Puzzle 8-25
Why was it unfortunate that the farmer hid his family's savings in a basket?

Clues: 1. The basket was out in the open. 2. Nobody stole the money.

Puzzle 8-26
Joshua divorced his wife after she showed up at his birthday party. Why?

Clues: 1. It was a surprise birthday party held at his friend's house. 2. His wife was not invited to the party.

Puzzle 8-27
Why was the teacher carrying around a pencil that read, "drop out"?

Clues: 1. He did not realize that the pencil said that phrase. 2. At one point the pencil had another strange phrase.

Puzzle 8-28
The employee was told that the product was flawed and to destroy it. He thought nothing of saving it and taking it home to be used. Why was he later arrested?

Clues: 1. The product was not hazardous. 2. He did not sell the product to anyone.

Puzzle 8-29

He decided to extract his own tooth because of a painful toothache. An hour later he went to the hospital. Why didn't he go to the dentist?

Clues: 1. He did not pull out his teeth. 2. He was in a great deal of pain.

Puzzle 8-30

The woman took her work home with her and later had to have her legs amputated. What happened?

Clues: 1. She did not work with animals or dangerous objects. 2. She contracted something from her work.

Puzzle 8-31

The two thieves ran to their getaway vehicle and jumped inside. They began moving but kept going in circles. What happened?

Clues: 1. They could not operate the vehicle correctly. 2. They were not on a merry-go-round.

Puzzle 8-32

Two pilots were flying, but they could not make out the traditional landmarks below, even though there were no clouds beneath them. Why?

Clues: 1. The landmarks were not obscured by anything. 2. They were looking with the naked eye.

Puzzle 8-33

A man boarded an aircraft and flew from San Diego to Portland, without purchasing a ticket. How?

Clues: 1. He was not the pilot. 2. He was not a flight attendant.

Puzzle 8-34

The Secret Service requested the artist's information and proceeded to contact him shortly thereafter. Why?

Clues: 1. The artist was not affiliated with any anti-government organizations. 2. He was not wanted for a crime.

Puzzle 8-35

The robber handed the bank teller a note that demanded $2,000 in cash. He left with the money, but the police showed up at his home within the hour. How did they find him?

Clues: 1. The robbery was not captured on film at the bank. 2. He was not recognized based on his appearance.

Puzzle 8-36

The thief stole a good deal of belongings from a wealthy home, but he was very easily captured. What happened?

Clues: 1. There was absolutely no chase involved. 2. He got all of the goods into his car without anyone seeing him.

Puzzle 8-37

Under doctor's orders, the man swallowed a handful of nails. Why?

Clues: 1. This was not in medieval times. 2. The doctor was not trying to kill his patient.

Puzzle 8-38

While cooking the main course, the head chef slipped on the floor and the restaurant was closed down for two days. What happened?

Clues: 1. He was not the only chef on the premises. 2. The accident caused an even greater one.

 Fact

> Many great thinkers and philosophers had weird occupations, but those jobs did not limit their ability to do great things. Albert Einstein was a patent office clerk, Henry David Thoreau was a pencil maker, Wilbur and Orville Wright were bicycle mechanics, and Nikola Tesla was a ditch digger.

Puzzle 8-39

The fire crew notified the police department that their nuclear alert was reading high levels of radioactivity. It was traced to a vehicle, but the policemen found nothing nuclear in the car that the couple was driving. What happened?

Clues: 1. The couple was on the way home from an appointment. 2. The couple was released to go home.

Puzzle 8-40

Criminals favored the poison arsenic because it actually already exists in small traces in the human body. Looking for a way to catch murderers, English chemist James Marsh was able to develop a technique to reveal an arsenic poisoning. What was it?

Clues: 1. He could test for arsenic on corpses. 2. Arsenic left unique traces.

Puzzle 8-41

She went to work and found that she was two inches taller. How did that happen?

Clues: 1. She did not wear shoes with added height for her job. 2. She was not stretched or pulled in any way.

Puzzle 8-42

He didn't want his job mentioned on his epitaph, so he wrote the words himself. His position was a significant achievement, so why did he not want it acknowledged?

Clues: 1. He was not trying to hide anything from those around him. 2. He did not accidentally forget to add the wording.

Puzzle 8-43

She passed the bar and wanted to become a lawyer, but the state forbid her from practicing law. Why?

Clues: 1. She did not have a criminal record. 2. A few years prior she would have been eligible to work.

Puzzle 8-44

The employee was fired after the butterfly exhibit opened and several butterflies died. What did he do?

Clues: 1. He did not kill them intentionally. 2. He had done something months before that caused their death.

Puzzle 8-45

The thief gave the bank teller a note, declaring that he wanted $25,000 in cash. The teller ignored him, even though he was waving a gun. Why?

Clues: 1. The thief was carrying a real gun. 2. The bank teller read the note and called the police.

Puzzle 8-46
He hit only three golf balls that day, before turning around and going home. Why didn't he finish his game?

Clues: 1. He was an amateur golf player. 2. He was not frustrated or upset with his game.

Puzzle 8-47
Without using satellite technology, they sent a message skyward knowing that it would reach its intended recipient. How?

Clues: 1. There was nobody in the sky to receive the message. 2. They were not sending out a message in search of intelligent life forms.

Puzzle 8-48
The photographer was looking through his video camera when he noticed a small, moving object. He shrugged it off as a small distraction and continued to shoot the film. He should have been more concerned because he was attacked moments later. What happened?

Clues: 1. It was not a small object. 2. There was no swarm or stings involved.

Puzzle 8-49
The laboratory performed an autopsy on the mouse and sent the results to the doctor who had requested the test. The doctor called his patient to congratulate her. Why?

Clues: 1. His patient was relatively wealthy. 2. She wanted quick results to confirm or deny her condition.

Puzzle 8-50
After his baseball team won the game, Thomas, the star pitcher, ran onto the field. Why did the crowd begin to "boo" him?

Clues: 1. The crowd was from his home city. 2. He was being disruptive.

Puzzle 8-51
The politician held a news conference days before the election. He was startled when one reporter asked him to account for some quotes that he had made during an event that took place the day before. He did not actually say the words that he was being accused of, so why didn't he deny the allegations?

Clues: 1. There was film of him speaking the accused words. 2. He could get in trouble if he told the truth.

Puzzle 8-52

The cemetery announced that it would soon be ideal for environmentally conscious people. What were they going to do?

Clues: 1. They were looking to save space. 2. The cemetery was going to be very basic.

Puzzle 8-53

The thief found himself in prison without a trial—in fact, he was never charged with committing the crime. What happened?

Clues: 1. He did not intend to go to prison. 2. He was later charged with the crime.

Puzzle 8-54

Each year, the teacher had to change the majority of his materials to distribute to the class. Why?

Clues: 1. He wanted his students to have the most up-to-date knowledge. 2. He did not believe they were using the material from the previous year to cheat.

Puzzle 8-55

The salesman left the restaurant with his client and ushered him back to his office. As they walked along the street, the client leaned over and asked the salesman if he had paid for the meal. The salesman assured him that he had. Why was the client unsure?

Clues: 1. The client had seen him hand back the bill. 2. The client wanted to make sure that the meal was paid for.

Puzzle 8-56

Each day he went to work he had to spend a portion of the day underwater. He was not a swim instructor or pool technician. What did he do?

Clues: 1. He was not in the Navy or Marines. 2. The water was meant to teach him something.

Puzzle 8-57

He received the Nobel Prize even though he was not awarded the honor that year. Why did he get it?

Clues: 1. It was under his name—he was not picking it up for someone else. 2. He was not the only recipient of the honor.

Puzzle 8-58

The priest was angry at the number of disruptions that occurred while he was giving his sermon each Sunday. He implemented new technology without telling the parish, but it backfired on him. How?

Clues: 1. The parish members did not find out what the priest had installed. 2. Members were more mobile and distracted now.

Puzzle 8-59
Jordan was late for an appointment, so he added his car to the others parked illegally in front of the building. When he came outside, his car was the only one without a ticket. Why?

Clues: 1. The cars were ticketed after he went into the building. 2. There was nothing special about his vehicle.

Puzzle 8-60
A local business had a sign created to advertise their company name. The installers placed the sign ten feet above the ground so that it would be visible from all areas. Two days later they were asked to lower the sign to half of its original height, even though it was much less visible. Explain?

Clues: 1. The sign contained other information. 2. The business catered to a select group of people.

Chapter 9
Puzzling Deaths

Death and dying are perfect topics for lateral thinking puzzles. People die in all sorts of mysterious ways, and these puzzles require you to think outside the scope of the traditional deaths you hear about on the news. The puzzles in this chapter involve murder, intent to kill, suicide, and accidental deaths. Due to their somewhat gruesome and graphic nature, it is suggested that you solve these puzzles in a well-lit and well-populated area!

Puzzle 9-1

A man went walking on a sunny day. He fell down, but wasn't found for five months. Why?

Clues: 1. The weather had been sunny for a week. 2. He fell in a hole and couldn't get back out.

Puzzle 9-2

She was unable to get pregnant and died shortly thereafter. Why?

Clues: 1. She did not intentionally commit suicide. 2. She was not murdered.

Puzzle 9-3

She picked up her glass, took one last sip, and died. How?

Clues: 1. It wasn't poisonous. 2. The contents of the glass were the cause.

 Fact

In the Victorian era, when a child died, the parents would ask to have a photograph taken to preserve the memory for as long as possible. Many pictures of sleeping children are actually of children who had died and were photographed in peaceful poses. Some parents would pose with their child for one last family portrait.

Puzzle 9-4
Her choice of window coverings sent her to prison. Why?

Clues: 1. She was not violating any homeowners' association rules. 2. The blinds were not used as weapons.

Puzzle 9-5
The salad ultimately caused Leslie's demise. How?

Clues: 1. She did not eat any of the salad. 2. She was not allergic to any of the ingredients in the salad.

Puzzle 9-6
If she hadn't read the story that day, her grandchildren might still be alive. Why?

Clues: 1. It was a short story. 2. She recognized someone because of what she read.

Puzzle 9-7
If his children had not been in such a hurry, they would have received a good deal of money upon their father's death. Why?

Clues: 1. The father suspected that they wanted the money. 2. The children were anxious for his death.

Puzzle 9-8
As Nadine lay in the hospital dying, she struggled with what everyone was saying to her. She finally gave up hope, but was able to pass away peacefully. How?

Clues: 1. She could hear, but was having a tough time communicating. 2. She was desperate to find a solution that worked.

Puzzle 9-9
He drained his pool on Friday, but was found dead at the bottom the following week. What happened?

Clues: 1. He was not murdered. 2. It was an indoor pool.

 Fact

> Jean Rostand, a French writer and biologist, is quoted as saying, "Kill a man, and you are a murderer. Kill millions of men, and you are a conqueror. Kill them all, and you are a god."

Puzzle 9-10
Two men were riding down the street on motorcycles. The one in back swerved and stopped in shock as he watched his friend's head become severed. What happened?

Clues: 1. The second man saw something in the air and swerved to avoid it. 2. The first driver was admiring the colorful birds in the sky.

Puzzle 9-11

They were living together and she suspected him of cheating on her. She looked in his wallet and he was arrested shortly thereafter. Why?

Clues: 1. She found incriminating evidence. 2. He kept the evidence because he was pleased with what he had done.

Puzzle 9-12

Charges were dropped against the man when he turned in his mother's pacemaker. Why?

Clues: 1. He had taken the pacemaker without permission, although his mother did not care. 2. He did his own surgery to remove the medical device.

Puzzle 9-13

She killed herself in the hope of helping her children. Why?

Clues: 1.She was attempting to donate parts of her body to them. 2. They were in no risk of dying.

Puzzle 9-14

He wanted to die but he was unable. Why did the crowd around him become angry?

Clues: 1. They were not family and friends. 2. They were not expecting anything to be bequeathed to them after his death.

Puzzle 9-15

She became visibly upset when the men entered her house wearing all white. They were not physicians or in uniform, so why was she distressed?

Clues: 1. She knew the men who came through the door. 2. Their outfits signified a depressing event.

Puzzle 9-16

She knew that her brother-in-law was lying about her sister's death, and may have had something to do with it. Why?

Clues: 1. He said her sister had committed suicide. 2. The method of suicide was not possible.

Puzzle 9-17

The two brothers carried the corpse between them in the hopes of cashing in on his death. Why?

Clues: 1. They assumed nobody would realize the corpse was not alive. 2. They needed his fingerprint.

Puzzle 9-18

He escaped uninjured from the fire but died later that evening. What happened?

Clues: 1. He forgot to take an important item with him as he fled the premises. 2. He was staying in a hunting cabin.

Puzzle 9-19
The politician stabbed himself in the leg. Unfortunately, he hit an artery and bled to death. Why did he do it?

Clues: 1. It was an intentional act. 2. He was not trying to commit suicide.

Puzzle 9-20
The two boys decided to play fast draw with their fathers' pistols. They checked the clips to ensure that there were no bullets inside. Later that afternoon, one boy was found dead. What happened?

Clues: 1. The boy had died from a bullet wound. 2. They did not later add bullets to the guns.

Puzzle 9-21
The security guard did not defend himself when someone stabbed him in the chest. He was awake and alert, so what happened?

Clues: 1. He was not stabbed through the chest from behind. 2. He asked someone to stab him.

Puzzle 9-22
The woman shot and killed her husband, but was stunned to hear the results of the autopsy. Why?

Clues: 1. Her husband was in much pain. 2. She was given incorrect information.

Puzzle 9-23

Two friends were in the desert shooting beer cans competitively. The loser was the one to miss the most beer cans. The first man shot his first beer can successfully. The second man shot his beer can and missed. The first man was declared both the winner and the loser. Explain.

Clues: 1. They did not shoot any more cans. 2. The bullet did not ricochet off the can.

Puzzle 9-24

Charlie stood on the ground, taking professional pictures of people as they jumped from an airplane and parachuted to the ground. Dave, Charlie's friend and fellow photographer, wasn't paying attention and died right beside him. What happened?

Clues: 1. Nobody landed on him. 2. He was not entangled in a parachute.

Puzzle 9-25

The woman fell down the stairs, broke her neck, and died instantly. Why did her husband die within days of her death?

Clues: 1. The husband did not commit suicide. 2. He did not die of a broken heart.

Puzzle 9-26

He calculated the height of the bridge, chose a bungee cord accordingly, and jumped off. Why did he die?

Clues: 1. He was attached to the rope. 2. The bridge was over concrete, not water.

Puzzle 9-27

The actor's dream was to be famous and make it onto the front page of the Entertainment section of the news. One day it happened, but he wasn't happy about it. Why?

Clues: 1. It was not negative press against him. 2. He wasn't unhappy about the mention, either.

Puzzle 9-28

The glider pilots were forced to bail out of their aircraft when they ran into some bad weather. Their parachutes opened, but only one survived. How?

Clues: 1. They did not land on anything hazardous. 2. The parachutes opened while they were still in the air.

Puzzle 9-29

Two men were shooting guns in a duel. They both missed each other, but one of the men died. How?

Clues: 1. The bullet did not ricochet off anything. 2. The man did not die from a gunshot wound.

Ⓔ *Essential*

In solving lateral thinking puzzles, it's often necessary to put yourself in the situation and think like the characters do. When it comes to murderous intent and suicidal tendencies, that's not an easy task to accomplish. You'll have to stretch your imagination and walk that line of desperation and criminal intent.

Puzzle 9-30
When the police arrived at the scene of the accident, the dead man was already entombed. How?

Clues: 1. He was not buried alive. 2. He was not buried by anyone else.

Puzzle 9-31
A couple had an argument and the girlfriend made multiple attempts to make amends. The boyfriend tried to drown out her talking by putting a pillow over his head and falling asleep. The next morning he was charged with murder. Why?

Clues: 1. He did not put a pillow over her head. 2. He did not intentionally kill her.

Puzzle 9-32
The groom's family acknowledged the wedding with traditional background music, causing two of the guests to die. Why?

Clues: 1. The guests did not die from heart attacks. 2. They did not dance to exhaustion.

Puzzle 9-33
The man decided that he wanted to be a pumpkin for Halloween. He had no idea that his costume would be fatal. What happened?

Clues: 1. He was not murdered. 2. He painted himself orange.

Puzzle 9-34
George walked fully dressed into the river. He could have taken off his clothes, but he refused to do it and ultimately drowned. Why wouldn't he remove them?

Clues: 1. He also had items in his pockets that he refused to remove. 2. He was in a hurry.

Puzzle 9-35
Cathy dropped her new purse down the hill and climbed down to retrieve it. She had no idea that it would cause her untimely death. What happened?

Clues: 1. Cathy could not get back up the hill. 2. Others were around and tried to assist her.

Puzzle 9-36

The nurse fed her patient breakfast and was later charged with murder. The food was not poisoned, or was the patient allergic to any food products. How did the patient die?

Clues: 1. The nurse purposely fed the patient the food that caused her death. 2. The nurse was actually not a registered care facilitator.

Puzzle 9-37

Had the parents let the police conduct the search for their missing child on their own, their child might have lived. Why?

Clues: 1. The parents drove around for hours looking for the child. 2. The parents finally found the child.

Puzzle 9-38

The detectives and police passed right over the body. It wasn't buried, so why didn't they see it the first time they looked?

Clues: 1. The body was underneath something. 2. Others touched the body before the police discovered it.

Puzzle 9-39

Carmen's husband, Steven, died of a heart attack after they had been married for many years. One day, a few months later, she received a small package in the mail. She opened the package, pulled out the tiny stone inside, and said "Hello, Steven." Why?

Clues: 1. Steven had not sent her the stone. 2. Steven was still deceased.

Puzzle 9-40

Tanya smothered her baby but was not arrested. Why?

Clues: 1. Tanya was possessive and very overprotective. 2. This was not the first baby she had smothered.

Puzzle 9-41

She wouldn't have died if she had arrived at school on time. What happened?

Clues: 1. The teachers were attempting to discourage tardiness at the school. 2. This was the first time she was late.

Puzzle 9-42

Tommy sat down to reason with his best friend, James. James was acting suicidal and at one point pulled out a gun. Tommy told him to put the rifle away and James shot him dead. There was only one bullet in the gun, so how did James kill himself?

Clues: 1. James killed himself with a gun. 2. There was not another gun in the room.

Puzzle 9-43

The housewife forgot to turn her watch ahead for daylight saving time and then committed suicide. Why?

Clues: 1. She was mortified at having not reset her watch. 2. She showed up late for a task she viewed as extremely important.

Puzzle 9-44

Charlotte was buried alive to preserve her decency. Why?

Clues: 1. Charlotte was not a prostitute. 2. She had committed a crime.

Puzzle 9-45

Rachel had a bad habit of chewing on her hair. Why did she die?

Clues: 1. She did not ingest any chemicals. 2. She went to the hospital for surgery.

Puzzle 9-46

The two men rowed out to the middle of the lake to catch some fish. They lay back and relaxed, waiting for the fish to appear. Only one friend made it back to shore alive. Why?

Clues: 1. One friend did not kill the other. 2. The friend swam back to shore.

Puzzle 9-47

He boarded the airplane and died during the flight, but nobody seemed to notice. Why?

Clues: 1. He died quietly. 2. He did not pay for a ticket.

Puzzle 9-48

A family was driving in a convertible through the country-side when a bird dropping killed one of them. How?

Clues: 1. It did not cause a car accident. 2. It landed on the seat next to a child.

Puzzle 9-49

A British magazine determined that bird-watching may be a hazardous hobby. Why?

Clues: 1. The birds did not harm the watchers. 2. Nothing fell on them as they were looking upward.

Puzzle 9-50

The man killed himself and then buried the weapon. He wasn't concerned about what people would think of it, so why did he bury it?

Clues: 1. He did not plan on hiding the weapon. 2. It was buried in the ground.

Puzzle 9-51

Isadora climbed into the open automobile and asked the driver to take her to her hotel. Had she chosen a car with a roof, she might have survived the drive. Why?

Clues: 1. Nothing fell on her. 2. She was not shot or beheaded.

Puzzle 9-52

The prisoner attempted to cleanse himself of the devil by devouring all things religious. Why did he die?

Clues: 1. He committed suicide. 2. He was placed in an isolated cell with no personal belongings.

Puzzle 9-53

If she had lain down and stayed still, she would not have died. What happened?

Clues: 1. She was alone at the time. 2. She wanted to clean up the mess.

Puzzle 9-54
They cheered when he died, even though they liked him. Why?

Clues: 1. He died quickly. 2. He was not murdered.

Puzzle 9-55
When the man died, many of his neighbors had a renewed faith in their religion. Why?

Clues: 1. The man was a criminal. 2. His death was accidental.

Puzzle 9-56
After a car accident, many people say that they wish they had left their house a few minutes earlier, or later, than they did. Laurie wished she had left five minutes later, but she was not involved in a car accident. How did she die?

Clues: 1. Laurie was driving. 2. Laurie was running behind schedule.

Puzzle 9-57
The teenager lounged by the pool reading a book. She took a swallow of water before realizing ants had climbed inside the cup. She died a few hours later. Why?

Clues: 1. The ants did not kill her. 2. She was quite upset and wanted the ants out.

Puzzle 9-58

There was a note lying beside the dead woman that said she was "extremely happy." What happened?

Clues: 1. She committed suicide. 2. She wrote the note.

Puzzle 9-59

Having buried his wife years ago, Frank's sister was surprised when she received a phone call to accompany him to the cemetery. While there, Frank had the cemetery dig up his wife's remains and he placed a new container inside the grave. Why?

Clues: 1. He was extremely upset during the swap. 2. He threw out the old container.

Chapter 10
Obscure Facts

Did you know that Albert Einstein was once offered the presidency of Israel? Or that Benjamin Franklin disliked the eagle as the choice to represent the United States, and preferred the turkey instead? These are the types of odd facts that make up the bulk of the puzzles in this chapter. In the first thirty puzzles you'll learn about many bizarre facts in situational puzzles. The final thirty puzzles are "quickie" puzzles that force you to think quickly and precisely to determine the solution.

Puzzle: 10-1
He was born, lived a full life, and died the day after he was born. How is this possible?

Clues: 1. It was the same year. 2. He wasn't human.

Puzzle 10-2
She walked along the riverbank, hoping not to get pregnant. Why?

Clues: 1. She was looking for something to prevent pregnancy. 2. This took place quite a while ago.

Puzzle: 10-3
While out camping on a spring day, Maria was able to accurately guess the temperature without using a thermometer. How?

Clues: 1. She listened to the sounds around her. 2. She could not tell based on the warmth of the air around her.

Puzzle: 10-4
Without receiving information or clues from anyone, he knew exactly where she was and traveled seven straight miles to see her.

Clues: 1. He was not human. 2. He was looking to mate.

Puzzle: 10-5
Not one of the customers found it odd when she added salt to their beverages. Why?

Clues: 1. She was not serving margaritas with a salt rim. 2. It was not a saltwater solution to gargle.

Puzzle: 10-6
Years later, Thomas was angry with his mother when he found out he had eaten his vegetables for no good reason. Why had his mother made him eat them?

Clues: 1. Her excuse was no longer valid. 2. She had been unaware of the mistake when Thomas was younger.

Puzzle: 10-7
All of Jane's friends called Sally a twit. Jane went home crying to her mom, but her mom told her that there was no reason to be offended. Why?

Clues: 1. Sally was used to being called a twit. 2. Sally liked any attention.

Puzzle 10-8
The company decided to make their product extremely foul smelling. Why?

Clues: 1. The company wanted to better aid the consumer. 2. The smell was to alert customers.

Alert!

When playing in a group setting, pay close attention to the questions that others are asking and the corresponding answers. Keep an open mind and process the information and clues together. When it is your turn to ask a question, be creative and gather as much data as possible while still abiding by the rules of the game.

Puzzle 10-9

Tracy was a witness for the defense in a murder trial. The prosecuting attorney asked her questions regarding the day of the murder, and at one point requested that she identify the time when she had last seen the accused on that day. When Tracy said noon, the attorney called her a liar, basing it on her previous testimony. Why?

Clues: 1. Her previous testimony had not discussed time. 2. Tracy had been lying.

Puzzle 10-10

The child insisted that the Grand Canyon was in Colorado and even brought his teacher documentation to prove it. Explain.

Clues: 1. An independent establishment of the United States government printed the documentation. 2. The documentation was later revealed as incorrect.

Puzzle 10-11
Nobody seemed to care that Janice kept sticking her feet in her food. Why?

Clues: 1. They saw her do it. 2. They did not eat the food.

Puzzle 10-12
Louise was pregnant in 1999, 2000, and 2001. She now has only one healthy child. She did not miscarry, or give a child up for adoption. How is this possible?

Clues: 1. Her pregnancy was normal in every way. 2. Louise is not human.

Puzzle 10-13
Jeremy and Joshua traveled to the moon in a space shuttle, where they died a slow death. What happened?

Clues: 1. They tried to eat but could not. 2. They were not human.

Puzzle 10-14
Kevin's family celebrated twenty birthdays on January 1st of every year. Why?

Clues: 1. Those who were being celebrated were not born on January 1st. 2. It was not a gathering to celebrate a bunch of birthdays in December and January.

Puzzle 10-15

Jonathan was sitting on his porch reading a book when the temperature quickly dropped by 20 degrees. The sun was not setting, or was there a cloud in the sky. What happened?

Clues: 1. Nobody was around. 2. The sun was still shining, although not as brightly.

Puzzle 10-16

Some people turn gray when they eat seafood. Why would one lucky guy turn back from gray to a flesh color?

Clues: 1. He was not ill. 2. He loved to eat seafood and incorporated it often into his diet.

Puzzle 10-17

The museum guards were not upset when they weren't offered a raise. In fact, they didn't make a salary at all. Why?

Clues: 1. They were paid through other means. 2. This took place in the past and the present.

Puzzle 10-18

She wanted to have children but did not want to carry them to term and go through the labor and delivery procedure. How was she able to have a child without recruiting a surrogate mother or using scientific intervention?

Clues: 1. She enlisted the help of the baby's father. 2. She did this procedure multiple times.

Puzzle 10-19
In most instances, a cloudy day means less visibility. In this particular case, if there weren't a lot of clouds, it would be less visible. What is it?

Clues: 1. This is not a light source. 2. Think large and distant.

Puzzle 10-20
Before going off to war he gently touched the frog in the hopes of an easy victory. Why?

Clues: 1. The frog was not a talisman of any sort. 2. He did not worship the frog in any way.

Puzzle 10-21
He was going home to visit his parents and passed over two time zones. Even though he was going to be there for a couple of weeks, he opted not to change his watch. Why?

Clues: 1. He did not bring a second watch. 2. He did not have to spend a lot of time converting the time change.

Puzzle 10-22
Martha was not mentally or physically impaired, or was she blind or deaf. So why did she take a service dog with her to the store?

Clues: 1. She was not training the dog. 2. She did not purchase the dog for another family member.

Puzzle 10-23

John was getting ready for his summer weekend trip with his friends. The day that he left, his mom helped him pack up his toiletries before getting his breakfast ready. He wanted cereal but she told him he could have pancakes instead. Why?

Clues: 1. She was not concerned with any digestion problems from the cereal. 2. She did not want him to have the cereal topping.

Puzzle 10-24

The doctor picked up the phone to dial his patient, but there was no dial tone. He checked the outside of the phone and fiddled with the wire. He checked for a dial tone again. This time there was a tone, so he dialed out. There were no downed power lines, and he had not fixed anything on his phone. What happened?

Clues: 1. Every line was turned off. 2. The system was shut down for a specific reason.

Puzzle 10-25

She accidentally slammed her finger in a drawer. Tears welled in her eyes, but never flowed down her face. She didn't wipe them away, so what happened?

Clues: 1. Nobody else wiped them from her eyes. 2. She did not squeeze her eyes shut to stop the tears from flowing.

Puzzle 10-26

He handed his friend a token inscribed with the words "Mind Your Own Business." Why wasn't the friend offended?

Clues: 1. His friend ignored the saying. 2. It was not a practical joke.

Puzzle 10-27

Cassie's dog began howling every time she stopped listening to the music. Why?

Clues: 1. It was always during one particular album. 2. The dog did not stop howling when the music was put back on.

 Essential

> Within many of these puzzles, you have to infer much of what is not being said. Inference is a mental procedure where you are able to reach a conclusion based on the evidence available to you. While reading the puzzles, you have to have a willingness to look for evidence that allows you to come up with a solution not expressed in the words.

Puzzle 10-28

Percy was a fickle fan of astronomy. He enjoyed looking through his telescope every once in a while, although each year, on the evening of his birthday, he made it a ritual to search the skies. He could easily find Saturn with its rings, but one year when he looked, he mistook Saturn for a different celestial object. Why?

Clues: 1. He was looking in the right area. 2. He was searching for Saturn.

Puzzle 10-29

Their annual payment was derived from a seasoning. Why?

Clues: 1. They knew nothing of the origin of the payment. 2. They were being paid for their employment wages.

Puzzle 10-30

She called the hospital to ask about maggots. Why?

Clues: 1. She was not concerned about them. 2. She was researching different hospital techniques.

Puzzle 10-31

What is unique about the word "Aegilops"?

Clues: 1. The answer does not lie in the grass. 2. The procession is rather important.

Puzzle 10-32
What is unique about the word "facetiously"?

Clues: 1. It is not the length of the word. 2. You'll find humor within the word.

Puzzle 10-33
What is unique about the word "checkbook"?

Clues: 1. Be careful where you're looking. 2. Flip through the pages to determine your balance.

Puzzle 10-34
What is unique about the word "skepticisms"?

Clues: 1. It's all in a flick of the wrist. 2. Don't doubt the answer is right in front of you.

Puzzle 10-35
What is unique about the word "swims"?

Clues: 1. Be careful doing acrobatics in the pool. 2. Synchronized swimmers are bound to get this answer quickly.

Puzzle 10-36
What is unique about the state of Maine?

Clues: 1. Besides the fact that it's the furthest east in New England. 2. Say it out loud.

Question?

What's the best way to solve the "quickie" puzzles in this chapter?

The majority of these puzzles require you to determine what is unique about a given word. You need to look outside the definition of the word and instead take a look at the makings of the word itself. Look at the pronunciation, the spelling, the order of letters, and the other ways that you could document the word.

Puzzle 10-37

What is unique about the syllable "ough"?

Clues: 1. It's not in the letters. 2. One sentence can clear up the confusion.

Puzzle 10-38

What is an octothorpe also known as?

Clues: 1. It does have eight parts. 2. You see it quite often.

Puzzle 10-39

What is unique about the letter "P"?

Clues: 1. Rhymes and pronunciations are beside the point. 2. Take a good look around you.

Puzzle 10-40
What is unique about the letter "J"?

Clues: 1. It's been left out of the mix. 2. Some day it might belong with the others.

Puzzle 10-41
What is unique about the word "set"?

Clues: 1. Set a good example and solve this one quickly. 2. It may be small, but it's got some power.

Puzzle 10-42
What's the best way to evade a crocodile when it is chasing you?

Clues: 1. Don't lie down and play dead. 2. Keep out of the way!

Puzzle 10-43
For humans, what is the most dangerous animal?

Clues: 1. Although many animals can maul you, they are not as dangerous. 2. These are apparent in many situations.

Puzzle 10-44
Who are Mizaru, Kikazaru, and Iwazaru?

Clues: 1. You know them better by their common names. 2. They might be based on a play on words.

Puzzle 10-45
What is unique about the word "receive?"

Clues: 1. It has nothing to do with the "ie" rule. 2. Even the most intelligent people get this one wrong.

Puzzle 10-46
Who are Dismas and Gestas?

Clues: 1. They are not as famous as their counterpart. 2. Only a select group of people will recognize the names.

Puzzle 10-47
What word can you add "in" to, but it doesn't change the definition?

Clues: 1. Some companies prefer to use just one of the words for safety. 2. It's an important tidbit to know.

Puzzle 10-48
How does one animal communicate with another animal that is hundreds of miles away?

Clues: 1. He speaks. 2. He is a loud being.

Puzzle 10-49
How many words are in the shortest short story?

Clues: 1. It's pretty short. 2. Don't forget that it needs all of the key plot points.

Puzzle 10-50
The original title "The Terror of the Monster" later became what famous novel and movie?

Clues: 1. The movie was terrifying for some. 2. It was not King Kong.

Puzzle 10-51
What is unique about the word "cabbaged"?

Clues: 1. Don't steal the answer away. 2. It's not a very melodic word.

Puzzle 10-52
The original title "The Sea Cook: A Story for Boys" later became what famous novel and movie?

Clues: 1. It's a classic story. 2. It's based on a trip to Scotland.

Puzzle 10-53
What is unique about the word "spoonfeed"?

Clues: 1. Don't worry about the double vowels. 2. Change up the view of the word.

Puzzle 10-54
The author thought of titling his book *Something That Happened*, but he later named it this.

Clues: 1. Something major does happen at the end. 2. The real title is based on a Robert Burns poem.

Puzzle 10-55
What is unique about the word "couscous"?

Clues: 1. It has nothing to do with the duplicate syllables. 2. Trying writing it in a variety of ways.

Puzzle 10-56
What famous novel had the working titles *Ba! Ba! Black Sheep*, *Tote the Weary Land*, and *Not in Our Stars?*

Clues: 1. It was later tuned into a movie. 2. The title that was used is based on a phrase used by a character in the novel.

Puzzle 10-57
What's the easiest way to explain the fear of fear?

Clues: 1. Use just one word. 2. Think in scientific terms.

Puzzle 10-58
What is unique about the word "proprietor"?

Clues: 1. The owner might use one of these. 2. The top floor is very useful.

Puzzle 10-59
What is unique about the word "uncopyrightable"?

Clues: 1. Don't copy the text. 2. Look beyond the definition.

Chapter 11
Fill in the Blank

Now it's time for you to fill in the blank. The puzzles in this chapter contain sequences that are missing an object or drop off after a few clues. Your solution should contain the correct answer for that object or be the next logical object in the sequence. The topics of these puzzles include history, geography, science, entertainment, and more. These puzzles are better suited for individuals because they cannot easily be solved using yes/no questions. Once you get started, you'll want to see what's next!

Puzzle 11-1

What comes next in this sequence:
7, 8, 5, 5, 3. . .

Clues: 1. Time is a valuable thing. 2. There are fifty-two weeks in a year.

Puzzle 11-2

Fill in the missing part of this sequence:
q, e, . . ., u, o

Clues: 1. You won't want to write to solve this puzzle. 2. This puzzle is not in alphabetical order.

Puzzle 11-3

Fill in the missing part of this sequence:
19, 13, 20, 23, 20, . . ., 19

Clues: 1. You'll find both time for work and time for play. 2. Full of cycles.

Puzzle 11-4

What comes next in this sequence:
1, 12, 16, 8 . . .

Clues: 1. Correct spelling is a necessity. 2. Look beyond the numbers.

Puzzle 11-5
Fill in the missing part of this sequence:
A, . . . , E, A, O, D

Clues: 1. History is important in this puzzle. 2. The order is important.

Puzzle 11-6
What comes next in this sequence:
1, 20, 7, 3, 12, . . .

Clues: 1. Read the paper daily. 2. Look to the stars.

Puzzle 11-7
What comes next in this sequence:
7, 5, 12, 14, 4 . . .

Clues: 1. Many people take it literally. 2. Look to ancient history.

Puzzle 11-8
Fill in the missing part of this sequence:
7, 5, . . . , 4, 7, 6

Clues: 1. This is a pivotal puzzle. 2. Mnemonics may prove useful.

Puzzle 11-9
Fill in the missing part of this sequence:
3, 6, . . . , 5, 4, 6

Clues: 1. It is an artistic array. 2. Be conscious of the weather.

Puzzle 11-10
What comes next in this sequence:
K, G, C, D, M, . . .

Clues: 1. Follow party lines. 2. This puzzle is the top seat.

Ⓔ Alert!

Beware! Some of the numbers used in the numeric sequences are not used mathematically. They actually represent the number of letters in a word or correspond to the placement of a letter in the alphabet. You might want to put together a quick chart of letters and their matching numbers for easy reference.

Puzzle 11-11
What comes next in this sequence:
K, M, R, C, M, . . .

Clues: 1. Middle English and Modern English. 2. A gathering of tales.

Puzzle 11-12
Fill in the missing part of this sequence:
C, O, . . . , D, C, P

Clues: 1. Contains all of history. 2. Plants and amphibians.

Puzzle 11-13
What comes next in this sequence:
7, 6, 7, 8, 10, . . .

Clues: 1. The order of this puzzle is important. 2. We all stand united.

Puzzle 11-14
What comes next in this sequence:
6, 9, 7, 6, 10, . . .

Clues: 1. It's not always about being the largest. 2. Location is important.

Puzzle 11-15
Fill in the missing part of this sequence:
18, 15, 25, . . . , 2, 9, 22

Clues: 1. An artist's array. 2. It might depend on the atmosphere.

Puzzle 11-16
What comes next in this sequence:
W, C, N, I, T, . . .

Clues: 1. It's really quite obvious. 2. You have to pay attention.

Puzzle 11-17
What comes next in this sequence:
B, C, N, O, F, . . .

Clues: 1. It all comes back to science. 2. Start somewhere near the middle.

Puzzle 11-18
Fill in the missing part of this sequence:
b, c, . . . , g, j, o

Clues: 1. You may want to jot this one down. 2. Sometimes straight just doesn't cut it.

Puzzle 11-19
What comes next in this sequence:
white, yellow, green, brown, . . .

Clues: 1. You'll find some Eastern influence. 2. Instruction is typically necessary.

Puzzle 11-20
What comes next in this sequence:
Ogden, Morris, Raymond, Lloyd, . . .

Clues: 1. These are last names. 2. The people are now deceased.

Puzzle 11-21
Fill in the missing part of this sequence:
d, . . . , p, r, p

Clues: 1. It's almost as important as your sign. 2. Mom will display it with pride.

Puzzle 11-22
What comes next in this sequence:
g, p, t, s, . . .

Clues: 1. Don't forget the date. 2. It's usually better than flowers.

Puzzle 11-23
Fill in the missing part of this sequence:
A, . . . , NA, SA, A

Clues: 1. Size is imperative. 2. Think big.

Puzzle 11-24

What comes next in this sequence:

A, A, E, NA, . . .

Clues: 1. You're looking for something different. 2. Birth to death ratio.

 Essential

If the answer doesn't materialize quickly, try various approaches. Apply the numbers to letters and vice versa. Look at the appearance of the letters. Solve the other puzzles to search for patterns. And as a last resort, view the clues!

Puzzle 11-25

Fill in the missing part of this sequence:

A, E, . . . , NA, AO

Clues: 1. The numbers matter. 2. Large scale.

Puzzle 11-26

What comes next in this sequence:

Australia, Greenland, New Guinea, Borneo, . . .

Clues: 1. Strength in size. 2. Land and sea.

Puzzle 11-27
Fill in the missing part of this sequence:
East Timor, Palau, . . . , Eritrea, Slovakia

Clues: 1. Youthful appearance. 2. Working backward.

Puzzle 11-28
What comes next in this sequence:
Illinois, Grand, Ohio, Ontario, Erie, . . .

Clues: 1. Pay attention to where you are. 2. Pay attention to where you start.

Puzzle 11-29
Fill in the missing part of this sequence:
Connecticut, . . . , Virginia, Tennessee, New York

Clues: 1. You'll always go in this order. 2. Method of travel is not important.

Puzzle 11-30
What comes next in this sequence:
d, e, d, c, b, c, . . .

Clues: 1. Think back to your childhood. 2. Play around with the letters.

Puzzle 11-31
Fill in the missing part of this sequence:
German, Irish, English, . . . , Italian, American

Clues: 1. Where did they come from? 2. It is not about languages.

Puzzle 11-32
Fill in the missing part of this sequence:
flood, earthquake, wind storm, forest fire, . . . , drought

Clues: 1. What do these disasters cause? 2. The answer is important to a lot of companies.

Puzzle 11-33
What comes next in this sequence:
Ford, General Electric, Shell, Toyota, IBM, . . .

Clues: 1. Do you own one? 2. Does somebody you know own one?

Puzzle 11-34
What comes next in this sequence:
New Guinea, Hawaii, Borneo, Taiwan, Sumatra, . . .

Clues: 1. They're not just exotic locations. 2. The islands are in order.

Puzzle 11-35
Fill in the missing part of this sequence:
Fairway, Midway, . . . , Franklin, Riverside, Centerville

Clues: 1. The post office often gets confused. 2. Multiplicity.

Puzzle 11-36
What comes next in this sequence:
p, h, h, o, n, . . .

Clues: 1. Pay attention to the signs as you drive. 2. Count as you go.

Puzzle 11-37
Fill in the missing part of this sequence:
n, e, . . . , w, a, b

Clues: 1. Many tribes will know what to do. 2. It is a respectful procedure to follow.

Puzzle 11-38
What comes next in this sequence:
2, 3, 2, 3, 4, 5, 6, 8, . . .

Clues: 1. You currently need a much higher number. 2. The numbers fluctuated in times of war.

Puzzle 11-39
Fill in the missing part of this sequence:
H, . . . , S, P, R, C, F

Clues: 1. You may recognize this from a high school science class. 2. Don't read from left to right.

Puzzle 11-40
What comes next in this sequence:
19, 13, 8, 5, . . .

Clues: 1. There are only five in this puzzle. 2. The order of the sequence is directional.

Puzzle 11-41
Fill in the missing part of this sequence:
7, 16, . . . , 18, 14

Clues: 1. The answer is more important to parents than children. 2. They only take up a couple hours of your time.

Puzzle 11-42
Fill in the missing part of this sequence:
D, P, N, G, C, . . . , M, S

Clues: 1. You may wish to take up coin collecting, if you don't enjoy this hobby already. 2. They all stand united.

Puzzle 11-43
Fill in the missing part of this sequence:
wife, child, . . . , cow, dog, cat

Clues: 1. You can read it in just one sitting. 2. Don't take them all with you.

Puzzle 11-44
Fill in the missing part of this sequence:
well, two, . . . , now, but, you

Clues: 1. It might be considered melodic. 2. No need to look beyond the first.

Fact

As you're trying to solve the puzzles, take notice that sometimes the letters listed are not the first letters of the words in the sequence. A few of the puzzles contain a different letter, although it is always in the same position for each word of the sequence. You won't see the first letter of one word and then the third letter of the next word.

Puzzle 11-45
Fill in the missing part of this sequence:
D, M, . . . , V, B

Clues: 1. From the queen to the pauper. 2. The individual ranking is important.

Puzzle 11-46

What comes next in this sequence:

u, d, t, c, c, s, . . .

Clues: 1. Your pronunciation shouldn't matter for this puzzle. 2. Depending on your location, it might be an easy solve.

Puzzle 11-47

What comes next in this sequence:

w, h, q, e, . . .

Clues: 1. It is a division of labor. 2. The sequence is increasing and decreasing at the same time.

Puzzle 11-48

Fill in the missing part of this sequence:

A, E, C, M, . . . , A, H

Clues: 1. You can travel between them. 2. Twice a year they change.

Puzzle 11-49

What comes next in this sequence:

F, E, V, F, T, . . .

Clues: 1. Computer files are the key. 2. Specific to an operating system.

Puzzle 11-50
What comes next in this sequence:
P, S, L, E, . . .

Clues: 1. *A Theory of Human Motivation.* 2. Deficit needs that can be met.

Puzzle 11-51
Fill in the missing part of this sequence:
M, S, T, J, . . . , M, M, S, J.

Clues: 1. Some might find this a musical clue. 2. The sequence often forms groups.

Puzzle 11-52
What comes next in this sequence:
I, E, G, . . .

Clues: 1. This puzzle stems from the 1600s. 2. You'll need an instrument to further view it.

Puzzle 11-53
What comes next in this sequence:
p, c, t, d, m, . . .

Clues: 1. Tragedy is the "imitation of an action." 2. Form of entertainment.

Puzzle 11-54

Fill in the missing part of this sequence:

r, . . . , b, q, k

Clues: 1. It is a medieval history lesson in the making. 2. Placement is important, but strategy ultimately determines the outcome.

Puzzle 11-55

Fill in the missing part of this sequence:

P, R, N, . . . , 1, 2

Clues: 1. Pay attention to the placement before moving. 2. With a flick of the wrist, it can change.

Puzzle 11-56

Fill in the missing part of this sequence:

RF, . . . , FK, FH, FL, ST, TK, TP

Clues: 1. Two words or first two letters of a word. 2. It is important to know when to get out.

Puzzle 11-57

Fill in the missing part of this sequence:

l, e, a, e, p, . . . , t

Clues: 1. It might be a foreign object. 2. Don't count your way through these clues.

Puzzle 11-58
What comes next in this sequence:
t, s, m, t, . . .

Clues: 1. Up, up, up and away. 2. You will never quite touch them.

Puzzle 11-59
What comes next in this sequence:
I, T, E, E, A, Y, M, . . .

Clues: 1. Hopefully you will see them through to the end. 2. Crisis resolution must occur and determines a positive or negative outcome.

Puzzle 11-60
What comes next in this sequence:
f, f, t, s, . . .

Clues: 1. The positions are important to consider. 2. A simpler answer than the others.

Chapter 12
Which One Doesn't Belong?

The puzzles in this chapter each consist of a group of words, names, or letters. Your task is to determine which one of these does not belong in the group. At first glance it may appear that they all work together, so you'll need to start thinking above and beyond the superficial meaning of each member of the group. Be careful when an answer leaps immediately to your mind! It may not always be the apparent answer that is, in fact, the correct one.

Puzzle 12-1

Which word does not belong in this group:

pear, hen, apple, ring, turtle

Clues: 1. It is definitely a seasonal item. 2. Think on context of verses.

Puzzle 12-2

Which word does not belong in this group:

ketchup, mustard, soy sauce, dressing, barbeque sauce

Clues: 1. It might taste good in another setting. 2. The colder, the better.

Puzzle 12-3

Which word does not belong in this group:

Maine, California, New York, Wyoming

Clues: 1. The cities are also important. 2. The size of the state does not matter.

Puzzle 12-4

Which word does not belong in this group:

date, rage, wear, pale, west

Clues: 1. Try to use your hands. 2. Do not write it down.

Puzzle 12-5
Which word does not belong in this group:
Paris, Rome, New York, Milan, Sydney

Clues: 1. It depends on which city you would like to visit.
2. Demographics play no part in this answer.

Puzzle 12-6
Which word does not belong in this group:
bell, jump, chat, door, bed

Clues: 1. It is often just a figure of speech. 2. The solution is often found in elementary school classrooms.

Puzzle 12-7
Which word does not belong in this group:
canary, dog, parrot, rabbit, hamster, pony

Clues: 1. These are special pets. 2. The family name is important to this puzzle.

Puzzle 12-8
Which word does not belong in this group:
liberty, venture, loyal, conquest, escape, endeavor

Clues: 1. Although a common thread seems to be patriotism and war, that's the wrong path. 2. You can drive yourself crazy with this one.

Puzzle 12-9
Which word does not belong in this group:
start, sharp, crazy, land, sofa

Clues: 1. At the end of the lane you might find an answer.
2. Stare until the solution comes to you.

Puzzle 12-10
Which word does not belong in this group:
bread, cover, trail, trade, friend

Clues: 1. The letter "e" is not the answer. 2. Don't lose it on this one.

Puzzle 12-11
Which word does not belong in this group:
Daniel, Jacob, Michael, John, Robert

Clues: 1. Do not look to the Bible for a solution here.
2. Names are a curious creation.

Puzzle 12-12
Which word does not belong in this group:
red, green, purple, brown, blue

Clues: 1. Hopefully something will give you a sign. 2. The bright letters should attract your attention.

ⓠ *Question?*

Why are the clues in this chapter so obscure?
The clues in this chapter and the previous one are more obscure because they are designed to be solved by individuals. The other lateral thinking puzzles are often solved in groups and the clues can be used to help get the yes/no questions flowing.

Puzzle 12-13
Which letter does not belong in this group:
a, t, f, r, z

Clues: 1. Pay attention to the right pieces. 2. Written or typed, the answer remains the same.

Puzzle 12-14
Which word does not belong in this group:
bull, fish, lion, giraffe, crab

Clues: 1. You might be drawn to one choice over another. 2. The animals say something about you.

Puzzle 12-15
Which word does not belong in this group:
tired, shy, jealous, delighted, sullen

Clues: 1. Childish innocence will help you figure this out. 2. These words are great at assisting.

Puzzle 12-16
Which word does not belong in this group:
knowledge, family, time, career, creativity

Clues: 1. You can bring these items into focus. 2. Eastern influences.

Puzzle 12-17
Which word does not belong in this group:
horn, doll, teddy, drum, elephant, boat

Clues: 1. Children love these toys as gifts. 2. It is a seasonal thing.

Puzzle 12-18
Which word does not belong in this group:
Henry, Romeo, Hamlet, John, Richard

Clues: 1. Think beyond the characteristics of the name. 2. The role is equally as important.

Puzzle 12-19
Which word does not belong in this group:
apricot, melon, orange, plum, apple

Clues: 1. The scents were never appreciated. 2. They were ground down to a pulp.

Puzzle 12-20
Which word does not belong in this group:
rabbit, buffalo, elephant, goat, dog, pig

Clues: 1. Lucky animals who got called to a meeting. 2. Personality influences.

Puzzle 12-21
Which word does not belong in this group:
elf, sole, rose, sofa, moon, donkey, pink

Clues: 1. They attempt to be educational. 2. German folk tales of enchantment.

Puzzle 12-22
Which word does not belong in this group:
Capella, Altair, Regulus, Jasper, Castor, Shaula

Clues: 1. Heavy names for an extremely light topic. 2. The puzzle is illuminating.

Puzzle 12-23
Which word does not belong in this group:
awake, zen, calm, energy, passion, refresh

Clues: 1. They do exactly what they say. 2. Name brand is important.

Puzzle 12-24

Which word does not belong in this group:

California, New York, Ohio, Texas, Florida

Clues: 1. You may have to push your mind to get this answer. 2. Location is not so imperative.

Puzzle 12-25

Which word does not belong in this group:

California, New York, Texas, New Mexico, Montana

Clues: 1. The area you live in is quite important. 2. Your house size should not matter.

Puzzle 12-26

Which word does not belong in this group:

California, New York, Florida, Texas, Illinois

Clues: 1. Are you sick of dealing with states? 2. Think smaller for this one.

Puzzle 12-27

Which word does not belong in this group:

Stone, Steve, Ed, Tim, Joseph

Clues: 1. They will never be done quite the same. 2. These names require some character development.

Puzzle 12-28
Which word does not belong in this group:
Moscow, Sydney, Tokyo, Toronto, Rome

Clues: 1. You have a sporting good chance of getting this one right. 2. It will not get quite as crowded.

Puzzle 12-29
Which word does not belong in this group:
Switzerland, Belgium, Canada, Denmark, Spain

Clues: 1. They have their reasons. 2. Working to fulfill mutual goals.

Puzzle 12-30
Which title does not belong in this group:
The Godfather, Peggy Sue Got Married, The Outsiders, Finian's Rainbow, The Great Gatsby

Clues: 1. One name ties them all together. 2. Different tasks for different titles.

Puzzle 12-31
Which word does not belong in this group:
heat, magic, jazz, dance, sun

Clues: 1. It can get quite hot when they get going. 2. Don't play around.

Puzzle 12-32

Which word does not belong in this group:
sneakers, trucks, eyeglasses, popsy, dedication

Clues: 1. A collection worth having. 2. Perfect for entertainment value.

Puzzle 12-33

Which word does not belong in this group:
pirate, glacier, arches, olympic, voyageurs

Clues: 1. Definitely a place to venture to. 2. It is time for a camping trip.

 Alert!

If you're stumped for an answer, try capitalizing the first letters of the words in the puzzle. The words as titles may assist you in visualizing the group differently and allow the words to take on an entirely new meaning.

Puzzle 12-34

Which word does not belong in this group:
Exxon, Ford, Chevron, General Motors, Chrysler

Clues: 1. Some do better than others. 2. Profit and loss is a major indicator.

Puzzle 12-35
Which word does not belong in this group:
tart, top, kite, hoe, low

Clues: 1. Each word has a beginning and an end. 2. Don't stop and move on.

Puzzle 12-36
Which word does not belong in this group:
pots, reed, tram, poor, ward

Clues: 1. An interesting way to read. 2. The correct answer does not involve the letter "r."

Puzzle 12-37
Which word does not belong in this group:
cleave, assume, crime, dust, skin

Clues: 1. It completely depends on the context of the sentence. 2. If you are ambiguous in your word choice, you might get an interesting response.

Puzzle 12-38
Which word does not belong in this group:
falcons, jets, condors, ravens, seahawks

Clues: 1. The fact that they can fly is completely irrelevant. 2. Find some way to gather it all together.

Puzzle 12-39
Which word does not belong in this group:
choir, dreams, criticism, hymn, serenade

Clues: 1. Not quite as relaxing as they might first appear.
2. You might need to read further into the choices.

Puzzle 12-40
Which one does not belong in this group:
arabian oryx, humphead wrasse, golden lion tamarin, gopher tortoises, black-footed ferret

Clues: 1. So few of them left. 2. What is the next step?

Puzzle 12-41
Which word does not belong in this group:
band, sing, aisle, chants, choir

Clues: 1. If spelled differently, the result would be the same. 2. English class comes in handy.

Puzzle 12-42
Which word does not belong in this group:
bloomer, volt, watt, bulb, saxophone

Clues: 1. An interesting spin on the name of the words.
2. Another puzzle where English class comes in handy.

Puzzle 12-43
Which word does not belong in this group:
display, buffet, minute, accent, present

Clues: 1. I think I know what you're saying. 2. It has nothing to do with a birthday or party.

Puzzle 12-44
Which word does not belong in this group:
travel, vagrant, chant, agile, needles

Clues: 1. It is a betting favorite. 2. Don't run circles around this one.

Puzzle 12-45
Which word does not belong in this group:
pioneer, Hudson, Galileo, viking, Magellan

Clues: 1. The answer involves expeditions. 2. It really is out there.

Puzzle 12-46
Which word does not belong in this group:
cat, dog, lion, sheep, horse, lamb

Clues: 1. It was left out on purpose. 2. History determined its fate.

Puzzle 12-47

Which word does not belong in this group:
play, skip, hope, care, youth

Clues: 1. A little bit of math might be necessary. 2. This puzzle is chock full of fun.

Puzzle 12-48

Which word does not belong in this group:
Sappers, Cells, Treasure, Loot, Mandalay

Clues: 1. Although these sound like Las Vegas hotels, they couldn't be further from the solution. 2. An early-nineteenth-century solution.

Puzzle 12-49

Which word does not belong in this group:
cat, ladder, key, salt, eyelash

Clues: 1. His beliefs could play a large part in this. 2. Be careful with your choice.

Puzzle 12-50

Which word does not belong in this group:
Nigeria, Angola, Italy, Ireland, Germany

Clues: 1. I'll time you on this one. 2. Keep your thoughts in alignment.

Puzzle 12-51

Which word does not belong in this group:
star, planet, sun, tree, bear

Clues: 1. Show your pride and heritage. 2. Don't blow past this one.

Puzzle 12-52

Which word does not belong in this group:
man, win, vent, wing, cake, key

Clues: 1. You need to leave something out of this one. 2. Start off with a bit of geography.

Puzzle 12-53

Which word does not belong in this group:
taste, chocolate, flash, legs, splash, spot

Clues: 1. A collector's more recent find. 2. Children and adults joined in on the craze.

Essential

In solving these puzzles you should first attempt to find a common bond between the members of the group. You can then begin to weed out some of the choices to come to a solution. If no commonalities exist, your next step is to determine why one of the members fits in with none of the others.

Puzzle 12-54
Which word does not belong in this group:
butt, pipe, firklin, double, runlet

Clues: 1. Let's make a toast. 2. Forms of measurement.

Puzzle 12-55
Which word does not belong in this group:
fool, devil, tower, sun, world, justice, castle

Clues: 1. Years ago the answer would remain the same.
2. Although directly related, it's not within a fairy tale.

Puzzle 12-56
Which word does not belong in this group:
Alice, celebrity, bananas, Manhattan, beach, September

Clues: 1. Part of the puzzle wore many different hats. 2. A
writer couldn't have done better.

Puzzle 12-57
Which word does not belong in this group:
best, square, tall, final, whole, mortal

Clues: 1. One of the tougher puzzles in the bunch. 2. Try
your hardest.

Puzzle 12-58

Which word does not belong in this group:
news, goods, phonics, mathematics, civics, billiards

Clues: 1. Be careful what you say. 2. Look at the words one at a time.

Puzzle 12-59

Which word does not belong in this group:
table, stool, eat, jump, silver

Clues: 1. It has nothing to do with eating. 2. Jump and bump.

Puzzle 12-60

Which word does not belong in this group:
balk, boot, chair, fall, net, sin, stable

Clues: 1. You may need a sporting chance. 2. Mix and mingle.

Solutions

The following are the solutions to all of the puzzles in this book.

Solution 1-1
George is a professional golf player and shot only two holes under par (getting an eagle). He usually performs much better.

Solution 1-2
The boy joined a band of criminals.

Solution 1-3
He was playing on a miniature golf course.

Solution 1-4
She lived on a street named Campus.

Solution 1-5
She was in the car but it was parked in the garage.

Solution 1-6
Catherine was two and dropped her sippy cup on the floor.

Solution 1-7
It was a two-way stop, but the signs were for the cars going perpendicular to the street on which he was driving.

Solution 1-8
Kelly was born on Leap Day and although she is turning 20 years old, she is really only celebrating her fifth birthday.

Solution 1-9
Maria drank everything before going back into the room with her father. When he asked for the drink, she would say that Mommy wouldn't get him anything. He believed her and walked into the kitchen upset.

Solution 1-10
These months contain Latin roots for numbers different than their placement on the calendar. For instance, *sept* means seven, but September is the ninth month.

Solution 1-11
Birds kept flying into the

window, falling to the ground with a broken neck. Her cat then dragged them into the house each morning after sneaking outside.

Solution 1-12

Marcia had asked for them! She wanted the special edition dolls to add to her collection.

Solution 1-13

She was trying to get her infant to fall asleep and hoped the soothing rhythm would assist in the process. After twenty minutes he fell asleep and she headed home.

Solution 1-14

It was seventeenth-century France, when most aristocrats wore high-heeled shoes and boots.

Solution 1-15

The driver was a student in a driver's education class. The passenger was the instructor, and he was equipped with an instructor's brake on the passenger's side of the car. The instructor used his brake when

the student lost control over the vehicle.

Solution 1-16

The building was a drive-through car wash and George drove through to get his car clean.

Solution 1-17

Kathleen's three-year-old daughter had injured herself and needed medical attention. Unfortunately, the car seat was in Kathleen's other vehicle, which her husband was driving. Kathleen did not want to put her daughter in the car without the car seat, so she called 911 to have an ambulance pick them up.

Solution 1-18

She was in the desert and kept seeing a mirage that she thought was water.

Solution 1-19

His dad was chewing gum as he drove his vehicle down the highway. After the gum lost its flavor, the father spit it out the window. Unbeknown to him, the gum flew back in the window in the back seat and got stuck in his toddler's hair.

Solution 1-20
The bird's owner carries him onto an airplane.

Solution 1-21
Casey was sneaking in late at night, past curfew. Her bedroom was upstairs and she knew that two of the stairs would creak. She took small, silent steps up the stairs and took large steps when she needed to avoid a particular stair.

Solution 1-22
It was Valentine's Day and she received many Valentine's cards in the mail.

Solution 1-23
There are eight people in the family. The mom, dad, five brothers, and one sister. Each brother had one sister!

Solution 1-24
Zero. There is no dirt in a hole, only air.

Solution 1-25
She is still in her mother's womb as she hiccups. They can see the rhythmic movement, but cannot hear the sound.

Solution 1-26
It was Halloween and one of the neighborhood children was dressed up as a spider.

Solution 1-27
The book was *The Complete Manual of Suicide* and she was worried that her son was reading it.

Solution 1-28
He had a bad conscience and returned the stolen goods, taking time to put them in their proper place and reconnecting electronics.

Solution 1-29
Her son was born with three of the fingers missing on his right hand. His left hand would be the dominant one in writing and the majority of other activities.

Solution 1-30

Time magazine named the computer as the man of the year for 1982, just four months after IBM introduced the personal computer.

Solution 1-31

A teenager had stolen a car and was attempting to drive out of Manhattan. He got stuck at the tollbooth with not enough change to pay the fee and a police officer became suspicious.

Solution 1-32

He said that she smelled like the rafflesia flower. This flower smells like rotten meat!

Solution 1-33

Tanya was filing for bankruptcy and wedding rings are exempt from inclusion among the assets in the bankruptcy estate.

Solution 1-34

He was typing out SOS in Morse code. SOS doesn't have any significant meaning; it was chosen because it is easy to transmit.

Solution 1-35

Her daughter was an infant and had over 300 bones. As she grew older many of the bones and epiphyseal plates fused together.

Solution 1-36

Their parents' bodies were in coffins, above ground, in a tomb. Therefore they were not buried.

Solution 1-37

The gold statue given out at the Academy Awards was named Oscar when Margaret Herrick, executive director of the Academy, said it resembled her uncle Oscar.

Solution 1-38

The man was a thief. When the police arrived he grabbed an antique sword out of the sheath where they were located on the wall. He moved forward to attack, but a policeman fired on him and he collapsed, quickly dying.

Solution 1-39

Fido. The name Fido stems

from the Latin word fidus, which means "faithful."

Solution 1-40

She was playing a game of Monopoly and had the dog as her game piece. She made it around the board, containing real names and locales of Atlantic City, in less than 20 minutes.

Solution 1-41

Edwin and Kitty Perkins ran a mail order business in the mid 1920s. One of the most popular products was a drink syrup called Fruit Smack. In order to cut down on shipping costs, they changed the syrup to a concentrated powder and sold it packaged in envelopes. The new product was Kool-Aid®.

Solution 1-42

They were going to Paris, Michigan, not Paris, France.

Solution 1-43

Catherine was late for work and faked the conversation on her cellular phone as an excuse. Mike knew she was lying because the particular client Catherine said she was speaking to was currently in the meeting room with her associates.

Solution 1-44

He asked for a bit. Prior to the Revolutionary War, some of the coins that the American settlers used were Spanish Dollars. These dollars could be physically cut into eight pieces, or bits. The customer wanted one bit, which is half of a quarter of the dollar.

Solution 1-45

The gift was a stuffed animal mockingbird. They had decorated the baby's room in a nursery rhyme motif and Jake bought a mockingbird from the "Hush Little Baby" nursery rhyme. Cathy hoped that after winding it up, the bird wouldn't sing so that they could move on to the next verse, the diamond ring!

Solution 1-46

Keri was a short-distance

runner and she was used to running with her head down. When she heard the gunshot outside of her window, she bolted out of bed and straight at the door.

Solution 1-47

Jennifer and Kyle went on their honeymoon and stayed at the Equinox, which is a resort and spa. It is a 2,300-acre resort that dates back to the late 1700s and has a rich history. It is a member of The Leading Hotels of the World.

Solution 1-48

It was Carmen's birthday. Her friends and family were gathered around the cake to sing her "Happy Birthday" and she immediately blew out the candle.

Solution 1-49

Theresa and her classmates were playing with a skipping rope. Theresa was at one end of the rope, chanting a rhyme. She began singing it faster and faster, turning the rope in time with the music until the bully tripped and fell.

Solution 1-50

He was on the beach of a lake, not an ocean.

Solution 1-51

Bob was a firefighter and was called to a fire that was burning in the apartment building next to where he lived. He was forced to break some windows to allow the heat and gases to ventilate from the building.

Solution 1-52

She received a package of Hershey's kisses packaged in a company mug on Administrative Assistant Day.

Solution 1-53

Harold's mother had recently passed away. As a bereavement gift a family member had sent him a small tree to plant in the ground in her honor. Harold dug a hole and dropped the budding tree within.

Solution 1-54

Stacy had fallen from the top

of a building and her friends knew that when she landed in the shallow swimming pool, she had died.

Solution 1-55
Charlie lived down the street from a slaughterhouse. Eventually the tenants moved to a different location and Charlie's neighborhood immediately began to appeal to new buyers.

Solution 1-56
They were bird-of-paradise plants.

Solution 1-57
He was duck hunting. He placed a decoy and was making duck calls when another hunter mistook him for a duck and shot him from across the clearing. It was deemed an accident.

Solution 1-58
Luke was asked to remove the pile of bricks that littered the outside of an old building. Luke thought the phrase was in reference to the building itself and he scheduled it to be demolished. When his superior found out he was furious and demoted Luke.

Solution 1-59
He was pricing engagement rings and knew that his fiancée wanted a pink or red diamond. He was very surprised to learn that a natural-colored diamond is rare and expensive, even though its hue is due to a color center resulting from deformation.

Solution 1-60
Shauna had recently undergone radiation for cancer and her salivary glands no longer functioned. She did not have any saliva, and unless you mix food with saliva, you cannot taste it.

Solution 2-1
The woman was pregnant and her water broke. Her husband left the office to go pick her up and take her to the hospital.

Solution 2-2
The daughter had been in a coma for three years and when

she finally regained consciousness, her voice had changed.

Solution 2-3

The woman was deaf and was
using a new technology that
helped her to hear certain
high-pitched sounds. When
the oven beeped, she heard
the sound for the first time and
began crying tears of joy.

Solution 2-4

The police went up to her
home and found that woman
had been looking through a
telescope. The vehicle she saw
was actually a toy car a child
had left in the sand.

Solution 2-5

He had decided to take a bath
before the power went off and
had filled up the tub. When
the power went out he went
upstairs, but he couldn't add
any water or the tub would
overflow.

Solution 2-6

Christopher was a cat and ran
when he saw the dog, Amelia.
He turned, ran off the edge

of the porch, and landed un-
scathed.

Solution 2-7

The man was a thief and was
stealing valuables out of the
trunk of a luxury automobile.
A security guard arrived and
knocked the thief into the
trunk and closed it until the
police could arrive. The thief
was escorted to the hospital
for slight injuries and then
arrested.

Solution 2-8

Tyler was a dog. He was hearing the dog whistle that a
trainer used at a park nearby.

Solution 2-9

Charles rode into town on
his horse, a mustang named
Mercedes.

Solution 2-10

She had a condition called
aquagenic urticaria, which
caused her to itch and swell
when she came in contact with
water. Instead of having her put
on gloves, her husband helped
by washing the dishes every

evening and putting the wet clothing in the dryer.

Solution 2-11

While the Smiths were on vacation, they left their computer on and their neighbor was able to watch their screensaver picture slideshow through his window.

Solution 2-12

He took a picture of the spider on his cellular phone to show his friends. The doctors were able to forward the picture to the zoo to determine the type of spider and treat the wound.

Solution 2-13

The newspaper headline that morning read "Grandfather of Six Hits Hole in One." The policeman did not continue to read the article about the golf tournament and instead thought he had hit a hole in his grandchild.

Solution 2-14

The girl was gossiping and lied about one of the guests. In Bogota, Columbia, where the two lived, a new decree was passed that calls for fines up to $150,000 for spreading false rumors. Citizens can be arrested for malicious gossip, which officials say have led to hate crimes and murder in the community.

Solution 2-15

Her husband had suddenly passed away the week before. He had ordered the flowers from the florist the day before he died, but nobody had called to cancel the order. The woman was shocked and began crying again at her loss.

Solution 2-16

They bought hole-in-one golf insurance. They were sponsoring a large golf tournament and giving large incentive prizes for hole-in-one shots at a few of the holes. The insurance purchased would provide the prizes if anyone sunk their drive.

Solution 2-17

The driver of the car suspected the driver of the truck of being intoxicated after watching him hit a canopy at a gas station. The man blocked the on-ramp to the highway to prevent the truck from causing injuries there. The police arrived quickly and arrested the truck driver on charges of reckless driving and driving while intoxicated.

Solution 2-18

The couple took a safari at the Wild Animal Park in California. Unfortunately, many of the animals were quarantined, so most of the animals they saw were local wildlife. The couple was angry because they saw these animals often on the land behind their house.

Solution 2-19

Timothy was looking at the reflection of the television in the window. The station was tuned to the weather channel and the images kept shifting to various weather reports.

Solution 2-20

In this real-life tale, a USC tailback had his mother's name tattooed on his chest, but her name was misspelled!

Solution 2-21

They were criminals and they were attempting to drill into a bank vault from a neighboring office. They miscalculated their measurements and drilled a hole into the restroom instead.

Solution 2-22

She went to have spa treatments at the local gym. In one of the treatments she received a linen wrap and was wrapped up in heavy linens and towels. She had a claustrophobic attack and ended up in the hospital for oxygen.

Solution 2-23

Her boyfriend had just broken up with her and she cried until she called her friend April, who proceeded to tell her that he had cheated on her and that it was a good thing that the relationship had ended.

Solution 2-24
They were driving in the car and he was naming off shapes he saw in the clouds.

Solution 2-25
He was donating money to the Salvation Army, but he accidentally placed a $20 bill in the bucket. He didn't want to rifle through the bucket and take it out, so he continued on.

Solution 2-26
The house was in a new development and the models had not been built. The area was in such high demand that he bought one of the homes having only seen the floor plans.

Solution 2-27
They were two children pretending to be knights on a merry-go-round at the state fair.

Solution 2-28
Casey bought him a shake with peanut butter from a local juice shop. They had only been dating a few weeks and she didn't know that her boyfriend was allergic to peanut butter. There were no ingredients on the Styrofoam cup and he didn't think to ask her what was inside. He had an allergy attack and sank to the floor of his office.

Solution 2-29
A new law went into effect that allowed library employees to kick out malodorous guests. Chad had extremely bad body odor and was offending the other patrons, so an employee politely asked him to leave.

Solution 2-30
She was wearing Mardi Gras beaded necklaces and he assumed she had received them by baring her chest.

Solution 2-31
The man had purchased one necklace for his wife, and an identical one for his mistress. He had each of them personalized with their names, but accidentally gave his wife the wrong piece of jewelry.

Solution 2-32

Kylie purchased three lemons, which perform all of those tasks.

Solution 2-33

She had taken him to the top of a local hotel for a nice dinner at the restaurant, but she did not know he had a fear of heights. He saw the view directly outside their table and began to have a panic attack.

Solution 2-34

Sam was a toddler who climbed on top of the island in the kitchen. He cried for his mother, who was upstairs putting his sister to sleep. He finally turned and climbed back on the chair he had initially pushed over.

Solution 2-35

He was transporting stolen goods, covered by a tarp. The wind blew portions of the tarp up enough that the products were visible and a police officer pulled him over.

Solution 2-36

Her son was autistic and she began a gluten-free, casein-free diet in the hopes that it would help him. This diet included knocking out all foods containing sugar. She saw a great improvement and for the first time he said, "I love you" to her.

Solution 2-37

He was playing poker and won with a flush in the suit of spades. The pot was $500.

Solution 2-38

The woman was dead and lying in a coffin. The son yanked the rosary beads out of her hands because his mother had recently converted to Judaism. He knew that she would not have wanted to be buried with them.

Solution 2-39

A woman had donated the plastic eggs after her grandmother passed away. Upon reading her grandmother's diary she learned that her grandmother had stuffed the eggs full of cash as an extra treat that year. It was a good deal of money, so the woman went to the thrift store to try to find the original eggs.

Solution 2-40

Her dog refused to drink tap water, so she fed him bottled water instead.

Solution 2-41

There was a sign on the toilet that read "Toilet out of order. Please use floor below." The man mistook the sign to mean the floor directly underneath the toilet.

Solution 2-42

Her cat got inside the house one morning before her neighbor left on vacation. She slipped cat food and ice through the letterbox to feed her cat until her neighbor returned.

Solution 2-43

Trenton had escaped from the prison a few years prior, but found life on the run to be extremely restrictive. He decided to turn himself in and finish out his sentence.

Solution 2-44

A fire was spreading from the outside to the inside of the house near the front door. The blaze caused a short in the doorbell wire, which in turn rang the bell. The family was alerted and quickly escaped.

Solution 2-45

She had filed for divorce and he arrived at the courthouse hobbling in on a pair of crutches. She knew he had been in a car accident, so thought nothing of it, until he dropped to one knee and fired at her with a shotgun that had been built into the right crutch.

Solution 2-46

They were stuck on the ski lift overnight. One of the staff members had turned off the machinery and gone home, leaving the skiers stranded in the chair overnight in freezing temperatures.

THE EVERYTHING LATERAL THINKING PUZZLES

Solution 2-47

Jonathan and his brother send the same card back and forth to one another for their birthdays. With each year they add a new line to the card before sending it back. Jonathan recognized the card front and knew his brother had sent it.

Solution 2-48

Kristine went to the hospital to be treated for a concussion after being hit. While there, doctors found a brain tumor that would not have been treated in time if she had discovered it at a later point.

Solution 2-49

They learned that many people were adopting black cats for satanic rituals during Halloween, so they put the black cats on hold until after the holiday passed.

Solution 2-50

Josh flew often on business trips and wanted to discourage people from talking to him on the flights. He flew mostly on Southwest airlines, which has an open seating policy, so he began wearing the surgical mask in the boarding areas and on the flight. Most passengers avoided sitting next to him on the airplane, and if they did sit next to him they didn't talk to him.

Solution 2-51

Some of the neighborhood children had offered her insurance to not egg or toilet paper her house on Halloween. She declined to pay them, and kept an eye out to make sure they didn't approach her house.

Solution 2-52

The president had passed away and many people thought numbers associated with his death would be lucky. They used the time, date, and age of his death.

Solution 2-53

Their mother was upset about the lack of gifts and quickly ran out to buy three scratch lottery tickets for her children.

234

SOLUTIONS

They scratched off the tickets and although two children won only one dollar, the third child won $100,000.

Solution 2-54

He was an inmate at a state prison. The prison officials did not want to pay the expense of guarding the inmate while he was being accompanied to the hospital and during his stay there for the surgery and recovery.

Solution 2-55

He had used a stolen credit card and signed his own name to the receipt.

Solution 2-56

The parents had been on a drinking binge and asked their son to drive them to the store. He was only ten years old and he ran into a tree. When the police arrived to investigate the accident, they arrested the parents on child abuse charges.

Solution 2-57

She had purchased a box of Lick 'n Crunch, created by Three Dog Bakery. All of the company's products are made with human-friendly ingredients, and the cookie was made with carob, instead of chocolate, for the pooch.

Solution 2-58

A day after eating homemade soup that contained chicken feet, he went in for a medical procedure that included an x-ray. After seeing the chicken feet, which looked like human finger bones, the medical examiner contacted a homicide investigator. A trip to the man's house resulted in the discovery of the chicken remains.

Solution 2-59

The state board stated that it was not handicap accessible and until the situation was remedied, nobody was to have access to the park.

Solution 3-1

He is looking at a new school of neon tetra fish that was placed in a fish tank with his beta fish. The beta is known to dine on the tetra fish and will eat them all.

Solution 3-2

It was a gravy boat, and all the gravy spilled across the table and the floor.

Solution 3-3

Long hot dogs should be cooked the same as short hot dogs.

Solution 3-4

The trunks were not at the car dealership; they were on an elephant farm, where he worked part-time on weekends.

Solution 3-5

He gave her a box of chocolates for a gift. When he said he would give her a ring, he meant he would call her on the telephone.

Solution 3-6

Bill was caught eating two "Grand Slam" breakfast specials at Denny's and his manager was upset because he wasn't following his dietary guidelines.

Solution 3-7

They were in a bowling league together and when they played on the day before Thanksgiving, he got a turkey, which means three consecutive strikes.

Solution 3-8

They were at a park and saw a group of ravens, which is called a "murder."

Solution 3-9

Jon had committed himself to a drug rehabilitation center. Andrea knew nothing about his drug addiction and was outraged that he had done this to her, so she called off the engagement.

Solution 3-10

He was taking golf lessons at a driving range. After driving many golf balls in all directions, he got angry with the instructor, and left for the day.

Solution 3-11

It was the cockpit of an airplane and they had died in a crash.

Solution 3-12
He was scanning through a document that his mother had sent him with his entire family tree. When he arrived at the bottom of the document, he saw an entry for his cousin's child, who had died as an infant.

Solution 3-13
A group of gorillas is called a band. Jonathan's dad sarcastically suggested he join one after a day of monkeying around.

Solution 3-14
She was getting sick of cookies on her computer. She had contracted a couple of computer viruses and was trying to clean off her hard drive.

Solution 3-15
He kept asking for a group of unicorns, which is also a blessing.

Solution 3-16
He was elevator surfing, leaping along the tops of elevators in the elevator shafts and riding them as they travel up and down the building. The teenager fell multiple stories and broke his neck.

Solution 3-17
The plate was a collection plate being passed through the congregation at church. Tony contributed to the donations, but did not get any food.

Solution 3-18
Henry stomped on home plate after running around the baseball diamond.

Solution 3-19
It was Carrie's dental plate used to artificially replace her missing teeth. She was using her tongue to play with a piece of celery stuck in it.

Solution 3-20
She ran into the store with her car, driving directly through the display window.

Solution 3-21
She was talking about a bridal shower event that she and a coworker were throwing for their secretary.

Solution 3-22

Lila and her mom were playing at the edge of the lake. Her mom went up to the house to make some sandwiches. She yelled out the window at Lila to watch the rowboat, which they had tied loosely to a tree. The wind had picked up and she said she would tie it more securely when she came back down. Lila was playing with her new skirt and didn't pay attention when the boat drifted out into the lake after the bow became untied. Her mom was angry and told her to go inside.

Solution 3-23

The word *deadline* also refers to a line around a prison or prison camp where prisoners would be shot if they crossed it. The definition originated during the American Civil War and the line was often a light fence or railing. Robert had to keep pushing back the deadline as more prisoners were brought into the prison that he ran.

Solution 3-24

The woman was attending her baby shower.

Solution 3-25

Steven was employed at a packaging company and he worked at too slow of a pace. His manager fired him the following day.

Solution 3-26

Carli had cleaned her daughter's dollhouse. Her daughter woke up from her nap, got a snack and then poured a full cup of grape juice onto the house. The juice dripped inside each of the miniature rooms, destroying the carpet within.

Solution 3-27

He bumped the nail with the cheek of his hammer and it went in at the wrong angle. He wasn't injured, but he was a little angry.

Solution 3-28

A parliament is also the name for a group of owls.

Solution 3-29

The musician was also a pilot and used the airplane instruments to navigate the plane to safety after the pilot fell ill.

Solution 3-30

The detective literally closed the case, a shipping case, with a person inside. He said that it was a suicide, but a person committing suicide (without assistance) could not have shut and locked the container while inside of it.

Solution 3-31

He was a troublemaker and his mom was insisting that he enter a new reform school to change his bad behavior. He had heard rumors about the school and was scared that he might be punished for acting out.

Solution 3-32

He won the case! He used a clause in the contract of the sale of his house to argue his suit and he won.

Solution 3-33

They went to an ear doctor because they suspected their son was losing his hearing. When examining the auricle (external part of the ear), the doctor could not find anything wrong with him.

Solution 3-34

She desperately wanted children and was very upset with the results of the tests performed on her husband.

Solution 3-35

The child had recently been in a car accident and was slipping into a coma.

Solution 3-36

The bin was full of diamond carets. He found them in a trunk when he was digging in the garden.

Solution 3-37

He was a guard in a castle and was taking food to the prisoners in the dungeon. He walked up to the grille on the doors and handed the food through the bars.

Solution 3-38
She was with him when he paid for his purchase. What she didn't know was that he was also picking up an engagement ring that he had purchased earlier.

Solution 3-39
She was awestruck at the balloons and decorations and for once sat still and stared in delight.

Solution 3-40
She wanted to make a statement at the black-and-white ball she was invited to, so she wore a flashy outfit and sent her husband in before her.

Solution 3-41
They were prodding the insect with sticks, forcing it to walk back and forth between them.

Solution 3-42
She was taking dance lessons and was told to galop, a popular dance of the nineteenth century.

Solution 3-43
It was an heirloom portrait of his grandmother, whom he never liked, and she didn't want him to destroy it.

Solution 3-44
Two other men who were accused of the same crime had been acquitted and found innocent. Those people testified against him in this trial.

Solution 3-45
It was her brother's birthday and she was making him a loaf of his favorite parmesan sourdough bread to bring to the party.

Solution 3-46
He was an altar boy at a local church and the priest asked him to dispose of the torn and dirty hymn books.

Solution 3-47
The knight had been spying on the two lovers as they planned their escape. He jumped from the wall and pierced Jonathan with a sword.

Solution 3-48

The captain wanted to retire and was anxious to find someone worthy of taking over his business. He met another captain while at sea and found him worthy. They both headed for land to negotiate a contract.

Solution 3-49

Christopher was playing cribbage, where the dealer's opponent is called "pone." Christopher was dealing and won the game on that hand.

Solution 3-50

The nocturnal animal was out searching for food. He bent to find a scent and was attacked by another animal.

Solution 3-51

He was driving a carriage when his horse was spooked. The horse began running quickly up the side of a hill and the rein was quickly slipping out of the king's grasp. If the end fell out of his hands, he would have no control over the horses. There was a cliff at the top of the hill.

Solution 3-52

He was trying to conduct business on his boat, but the buyer wasn't interested in closing the transaction.

Solution 3-53

He was playing a game of basketball and it was his turn to play and take away (wrest) the ball from the other players.

Solution 3-54

The class was tying knots and he had demonstrated the best knot to tie.

Solution 3-55

She was using fresh fertilizer as she planted her rows of seeds and it smelled terrible.

Solution 3-56

He was running through town, sounding the alarm with a bell (also known as a tocsin).

Solution 3-57

Timothy was disappointed because his aunt was unable to fly in for his birthday party.

Solution 3-58

The couple was getting married in a hot air balloon, but it was a windy day and the wedding coordinator had doubts that the ceremony would run smoothly.

Solution 3-59

They were traveling by train on vacation without their children. That night they found that their berth was small and cramped. It was a soft and smooth mattress, but they tossed and turned, trying to make room for one another.

Solution 3-60

A couple was attempting to get back into the United States from Mexico. One of the border patrol officers was female and she was very aggressive. She gave them a hard time and demanded an inspection of their vehicle because they were of Mexican descent.

Solution 4-1

Coca-Cola was invented when a doctor was mixing headache medication to taste good. The approval board found that the medicine tasted better than it worked, so they carbonated the liquid and then marketed it.

Solution 4-2

In 1881, Dr. Albert Southwick saw an elderly drunkard touch terminals of an electrical generator in Buffalo, New York. He was amazed at how quickly, and presumably painlessly, the man was killed, so Southwick described the episode to his friend, State Senator David McMillan. McMillan later spoke to Governor David B. Hill about replacing hanging with electricity for capital punishment.

Solution 4-3

Wrigley's Gum was the first product to have a bar code. The woman had heard on the news about the new bar coding system and knew that the item was the gum.

Solution 4-4

In 1946, Percy LeBaron Spencer of the Raytheon Company

found that the radar waves he was working with melted the candy bar in his pocket. Raytheon then went on to create the microwave oven.

Solution 4-5

In the mid 1800s, French chemist Charles Gerhardt mixed a chemical with salicylic acid and created acetylsalicylic acid, or aspirin. Unfortunately he decided that this new compound wasn't practical because it was difficult to create and took a lot of time. He set it aside, only to have it rediscovered sixty-five years later.

Solution 4-6

The University of Florida Gators football team credited their 1967 Orange Bowl victory with their new drink of choice, Gatorade. Dr. Robert Cade had developed Gatorade for the team, finally coming up with a concoction consisting of water, sugar, sodium, potassium, phosphate, and lemon juice. The team was able to play much longer in the warm

conditions when they drank Gatorade instead of water.

Solution 4-7

In 1921, a health clinician in Minneapolis spilled his patients' breakfast on the stove. The bran gruel cracked and sizzled into a crisp flake that was later perfected and named Wheaties.

Solution 4-8

In 1900, Swiss textile engineer Jacques E. Brandenberger first came up with the idea for a waterproof tablecloth while seated at a restaurant. He hoped to invent a clear, flexible film that could be applied to the cloth. He experimented with multiple materials, including liquid viscose. The viscose made the cloth too stiff, but it peeled off in a transparent film! Thus cellophane was born and in 1908 a machine was created to make sheets of the film.

Solution 4-9

Dr. John Harvey Kellogg and his younger brother Will Keith Kellogg were called away after cooking wheat at the health spa where they worked. When they returned the wheat was stale, but they forced it through rollers as normal. The wheat came out as a very thin flake, instead of dough, and when the brothers baked it they realized they had discovered a new breakfast cereal. Today, Kellogg's is among the most popular cereal producers in the world.

Solution 4-10

In 1970, Silver Spencer was an employee at 3M Laboratories. He was trying to develop a strong adhesive, but ultimately created a weaker adhesive than 3M was already producing. It stuck to products, but could then be removed without damaging the surface. Ten years later, 3M distributed the Post-It Notes nationwide.

Solution 4-11

There are many tales that describe the invention of the ice cream sundae, but they all revolve around a central theme—the sinfulness of the ice cream soda. The soda was extremely popular among teens in the late 1800s, but it was frowned upon by religious conservatives. The ice cream soda was eventually banned in some areas—either completely, or just on Sundays. The "sundae" was created as an alternative to selling ice cream sodas on days they were banned.

Solution 4-12

The invention of kites may date back as far as 3,000 years to China, and they were used for a variety of purposes across the years. In 1232, kites were used to fly messages over Mongol lines. The strings were cut, allowing the kites to land among the Chinese prisoners and inciting them to revolt and escape.

Solution 4-13

Raisins were most likely invented when the grapes dried naturally on the vine. The sweet treat that resulted led others to pick the grapes and lay them in the sun to dry. Other fruits were soon added to the mix and sun-drying became a great tool for preservation.

Solution 4-14

The most common story as to the origin of coffee stems back to A.D. 600–800 when a goat herder in Eastern Africa noticed that his goats were acting strangely. They were awake all night, jumping and leaping around. The goat herder realized they had been eating the red berries off of nearby shrubs. He, in turn, tried the berries and felt awake and invigorated. Later, a monk was passing through and was shown the berries. The monk crushed a few into powder and steeped them in water, creating the first coffee drink.

Solution 4-15

The children were repeating the nursery rhyme Humpty Dumpty, which is possibly attributed to one of a few historical events. During the English Civil War there was a large cannon that was mounted to the top of St. Mary's. It defended the city of Colchester against a siege in the summer of 1648, but fell off the wall and was unable to be mended. The nursery rhyme could also represent King Richard III in the Battle of Bosworth, when he was murdered atop his horse, or Charles I of England, when he was toppled by the Puritan majority in Parliament.

Solution 4-16

True story: Earle Dickson worked for Johnson & Johnson and his wife, Josephine Dickson, had an odd knack for cutting herself. Earle sat down one day with some gauze and adhesive tape, cut the tape into strips, and stuck a piece of gauze in the middle of each strip. Josephine now had access to the bandages whenever she cut herself. Johnson & Johnson heard of the idea and began mass-producing them as Band-Aids.

Solution 4-17

Louis Braille became blind at

the age of three from an accident with his father's tools. He attended a school for the blind in Paris, but the books there were bulky and cumbersome to read, as they only contained large raised letters. There were very few books on hand because they were expensive to make. Braille decided to shorten a raised alphabet code that was being used by the French army so soldiers could read at night without any light. He made up a new alphabet of combinations using only six raised dots that revolutionized reading for the blind.

Solution 4-18

In 1928, Walter Diemer worked as an accountant for the Fleer Chewing Gum Company in Philadelphia. In his spare time, he experimented with different chewing gum recipes. One day he came up with a batch that was more stretchy and contained bubbles. He had found the recipe for bubble gum.

Solution 4-19

In 1983, George Crum worked as a chef for Moon Lake Lodge's restaurant in New York. One evening a guest complained about the thickness of the French fries and asked for a thinner batch. After another failed attempt, Crum cut the potatoes very thin, too thin to spear with a fork. He had hoped to annoy the customer, but surprisingly the guest loved the order and potato chips became increasingly popular.

Solution 4-20

Elwood Norris recently won the annual Lemelson-MIT Prize for his HyperSonic Sound system. The emitter sends a focused beam of sound above the range of human hearing. When it lands on a person, it seems like the sound is coming from inside his head.

Solution 4-21

In 1767, John Spilsbury was a teacher in England. He cut out the counties of Wales and

England from a map that he had adhered to hardwood. He used his tool for teaching geography, but people began creating "puzzles" out of other pictures for entertainment.

Solution 4-22

Twinkies were originally sold without cream fillings for use in strawberry shortcakes. James Dewar, a bakery manager, thought of filling the Twinkies after strawberry season ended. Originally they were filled with bananas, but there was a shortage during World War II, so they began using a cream filling.

Solution 4-23

In 1948, George de Mestrall, a Swiss engineer, came up with an idea for a new fastener. He came home from hiking one day and discovered some burrs clinging to his cloth jacket. On further inspection, he noticed that the burrs contained many thin strands that could easily hook onto cloth or fur. He decided to implement this idea using two strips of nylon fabric. One side contains thousands of small hooks, and the other side contains small loops. He named this product Velcro.

Solution 4-24

In 1893, Whitcomb L. Judson patented his "clasp-locker" that consisted of a slide fastener that could be used with one hand. He created the fastener to assist his friend who had a stiff back and could not tie his shoes. It wasn't until the early 1900s that this hookless fastener took on the name "zipper."

Solution 4-25

Albert J. Parkhouse was an employee of a wire and novelty company. In 1903 he arrived at work to find that all of the coat hooks were in use. He became frustrated and took a piece of wire, forming it into two ovals that would fit inside his jacket shoulders with a hook on top to hang, hence, the hanger.

Solution 4-26

In 1821, Thomas Jennings

received a patent for his dry-cleaning process. He was the first African American to receive a patent, and he used this money to purchase his family out of slavery and further the abolitionist cause.

Solution 4-27

Several theories exist for why a pretzel is shaped the way it is. Most of the information states that the shape is a representation of a child's arms folded in prayer. Supposedly monks in France or Italy around A.D. 610 used the treat as a reward when children remembered their prayers.

Solution 4-28

Because the warmth of their hands on the glass would cause the mint julep to warm faster, people drank them through straws. The first straws used were natural grass straws, but they were cut from rye and flavored the drink with a plant-like taste. Marvin Stone, a manufacturer of cigarette holders, created a paper drinking straw to replace the grass ones, eventually using a paraffin-coated manila paper so that the straw would not dissolve in the liquid.

Solution 4-29

Thomas Sullivan invented tea bags in 1908 as a way to package tea samples. He placed the loose tea in a small bag of silk, and many of his customers brewed the tea in the bag instead of dumping the tea into a teapot. Tea bags were later made with a thin paper so that the leaves could steep in water.

Solution 4-30

Walter Hunt invented the safety pin in 1849 as he sat twisting a piece of wire trying to think of something to pay off a $15 debt. He had many other inventions under his belt and he didn't think highly of his wire creation, so he sold the patent for $400.

Solution 4-31

Richard James was a naval

engineer helping to develop an anti-vibration device for ship equipment. He knocked over some springs and watched them "walk" their way down the shelves. He showed his wife, Betty, who came up with the name Slinky and later ran the company.

Solution 4-32

The Remington typewriter in 1878 introduced a new idea: a shift key. Prior to this, typewriters typed in all capital letters. Some manufacturers chose to add the entire lower case alphabet to the typewriter, but Remington's solution remained the preferred choice.

Solution 4-33

Elisha Otis created a safety elevator that he demonstrated in 1953 at the Crystal Palace Exposition in New York. When he got to the top of his ascent, he asked his assistant to cut the elevator's cord. The platform stayed in place, due to the toothed guardrail located on the sides of the elevator

shaft that engaged to catch the car in the event of a cable failure. This invention helped in the construction of tall buildings, thus allowing people to ride up to the top and view the city below them.

Solution 4-34

In 1904, Mary Anderson applied for a patent for a windshield wiper that could be operated from the interior of a car. Prior to windshield wipers, drivers would have to periodically stop their cars to remove rain and snow from their windows. Anderson was teased and laughed at because of her idea, and many felt that the wiping motion would distract the drivers. She got the last laugh in 1913, when automobiles came standard with mechanical windshield wipers.

Solution 4-35

Mary Phelps Jacob created the modern brassiere in 1913 when she found that the traditional corset was visible through the plunging neckline and sheer material of a dress she wanted to wear to an event. She gathered two handkerchiefs and some ribbon and created a bra. She made the same garment for family and friends and eventually received a patent for the Backless Brassiere.

Solution 4-36

Frances Gabe is still fine-tuning her self-cleaning house. Each room has a 10-inch-square apparatus that soaps, rinses, and dries the room. She also has cupboards that act as a dishwasher, closets that act as a washer and dyer, and the sinks, toilets, and bathtubs are all self-cleaning. Gabe has more than 68 devices that she has introduced over the past 40 years to her house.

Solution 4-37

French physician Rene Laennec created the monaural stethoscope in 1816. He was embarrassed about having to place his ear to his female patient's chest (the method of auscultation at that time).

Instead, he rolled up some paper and placed one end to her chest and the other end to his ear. The sounds were louder and clearer than if he had his ear against her chest, so he created an instrument to replicate the cylinder.

Solution 4-38

The Roomba® vacuum is a robotic cleaner that vacuums a room, or portion of a room, for you. A group at M.I.T. created the handy robot and it is sold through iRobot today.

Solution 4-39

In 1912, Clarence Crane invented Life Savers as a summer candy because it could withstand the heat better than chocolate. The mints had a hole and resembled small life preservers, thus the name.

Solution 4-40

PEZ dispensers were originally designed to look like a cigarette lighter and contained peppermint-flavored candy (the name PEZ is derived from the

German word for peppermint). Eduard Hass, the inventor of PEZ, imported the product to the United States in 1952, but sales were low. He changed the flavors and the packaging, introducing cartoon heads at the tops of the dispensers for children.

Solution 4-41

WD-40 stands for Water Displacement perfected on the 40th time. Rocket Chemical Company finally succeeded in developing the current formula in 1953. Originally designed as a corrosive prevention for the aerospace industry, the product is now a household name.

Solution 4-42

Bette Nesmith Graham created Liquid Paper in her kitchen blender, looking for a product that would cover up typing errors. She colored a batch of water-based paint and used a paintbrush to apply it to any mistakes. Soon the secretaries in the office were asking for a bottle, and Graham happily obliged. She then started her own company, making millions on her invention. Although she left her previous employers, they were able to benefit from her product.

Solution 4-43

Jay Sorensen left a drive-through coffee bar one day and spilled his coffee in his lap. The cup had been wrapped in a napkin to protect a person's hand from the heat, but Sorensen took that idea and ran with it. He invented the Java Jacket, an insulating coffee cup sleeve.

Solution 4-44

Lewis Waterman ruined a contract for an important client when his new fountain pen leaked on the document. As he ran back to his office for another contract, a competing insurance broker closed his deal. He tinkered around in his brother's workshop until he came up with a pen that used capillary action to allow a steady, even flow of ink.

He also replaced the pen nib and added a clip to the cap of the pen.

Solution 4-45

Sylvan Goldman, owner of a grocery store chain in Oklahoma, created a shopping cart after watching customers struggle with handheld baskets. His first design was similar to a folding chair on wheels, with two baskets on top of each other. Initially, customers did not want to use them—men did not want to appear weak and women did not want to seem unstylish. But, after hiring models to use the cart and showing patrons how to operate the carts, they became extremely popular.

Solution 4-46

In 1915, John Van Wormer took out a patent on a new product called a "Pure-Pak." It was a disposable, paper container for milk. The idea came after he dropped a bottle of milk one morning, making a large puddle of milk and broken glass. He decided there had to be a better container. It took ten years to create a machine that would make the product, and another several years for the general public to catch on, but by 1950 his company was producing over 20 million cartons a day.

Solution 4-47

Thomas Fogarty introduced a balloon catheter in 1961 and helped mark the beginning of non-invasive surgeries. After watching the method of surgeries to remove blood clots, he devised a solution using his fly-fishing techniques. He tied the tip of a latex glove to a catheter that could then be inflated to drag the clot out of the body.

Solution 4-48

In sixteenth-century France April 1st was the first day of the calendar. When Pope Gregory changed the date to January 1st, many citizens were skeptical or unaware of the change. Those citizens celebrated April 1st as the New Year and others called them fools and played tricks on them.

Solution 4-49
Gerry Thomas, an employee for Swanson foods, developed the TV dinner as a way to use left-over meat from Thanksgiving. He used an aluminum serving dish and added the foods to their individual compartments. The tray could be heated and used as a serving dish, all in front of the favorite pastime of the 1950s—the television.

Solution 4-50
Leo Baekeland announced his invention, Bakelite, in 1909 and it was the first synthetic plastic. It was used alone to form objects such as records and machinery gears, or in combination with other materials as a laminate and surface coating.

Solution 4-51
In 1879, Proctor & Gamble had a mistake occur with their "White Soap." A workman in the factory left the machinery running during lunch, causing air to be mixed into the batch of soap. He poured the soap as normal into frames, and they were packaged and shipped to customers. Weeks later an influx of letters arrived, raving about the soap that floated, and Ivory was born.

Solution 4-52
In 1867, chemist and inventor Henri Nestlé created an infant product for mothers who were unable to breastfeed. When the formula saved the life of a newborn infant, Nestle began production of the product, Farine Lactée Nestlé, as the first baby formula.

Solution 4-53
Benjamin Franklin was near-sighted, but as he aged he found that he was becoming farsighted as well. He got tired of switching between two pairs of glasses, so one day he cut the lenses of both spectacles horizontally and made a pair of glasses that incorporated the lenses. It was the first pair of bifocals.

Solution 4-54

Conrad Hubert purchased the idea for a light-up flower-pot from his friend for a small amount of money. He modified the product, taking the battery, bulb, and paper tube, and created an "electric hand torch." He originally sold it as a novelty item, but the flashlight proved to be very useful and sales increased dramatically.

Solution 4-55

In 1947, Ed Lowe was approached by a neighbor looking for sand as a replacement to using ashes in her cat's box. He suggested using clay instead, and the neighbor raved about the absorbency of the clay. Ed filled up brown bags with clay and began giving away his "kitty litter" for customers to try. They loved the product, and in 1964 Tidy Cat was established.

Solution 4-56

In old English (approximately the fifteenth century), dishes and pots were made out of economical orange clay named "pygg." Housewives saved money in jars made out of the clay and called them their "pygg bank" or "pyggy bank." As the years progressed, the name was forgotten and when English potters obtained a request for a piggy bank, they created jars in the shape of pigs.

Solution 4-57

A railroad car full of poorly rolled paper, too thick to be toilet paper, arrived at the Scott Paper Company in 1879. Arthur Scott, head of paper products, perforated the paper and sold it as disposable paper towels to a nearby school. There a teacher had been handing out soft pieces of paper to students with runny noses, so as to not cross-contaminate the toilet paper roll. Eventually, the product was sold to hotels, restaurants, and businesses containing public restrooms.

Solution 4-58

During World War II, a synthetic pliable rubber was created

cheaply and used for a variety of small jobs including caulking and molding. When the war was over, there was a surplus of the material. Peter Hodgson, a storeowner in Connecticut, purchased a large amount, packaged the rubber in plastic eggs, and sold it to children under the name Silly Putty. They molded the rubber into a variety of shapes, lifted images off newspapers and comics, and the product is still a huge hit today.

Solution 4-59

The order of keys on a typewriter! The first prototype had two rows of keys in alphabetical order. The problem that occurred with this arrangement was when keys close to one another were hit in succession, they clashed and jammed together. Christopher Latham Sholes worked out a system that arranged the keys of common letter pairs so that their typebars hung at safe distances from one another.

The system took some learning, but even with advances in technology, the letter order has stayed the same.

Solution 4-60

Cracker Jack. In 1896, Louis Rueckheim had discovered a way to keep molasses-covered popcorn from sticking together and offered the treat to a salesman. The salesman said "that's crackerjack!" which was slang for something really good. Louis's brother, F. W., had the words trademarked.

Solution 4-61

It was an ice cream cone. Some historians say that Charles Menches was selling ice cream during the Louisiana Purchase Exposition in St. Louis. It was August, 1904, and ice cream was still served in dishes, but Charles ran out of his dishes by noon. He thought quickly, buying some Zalabia, a Middle Eastern treat consisting of a wafer-like pastry, from his friend. He rolled the Zalabia into a cone shape and scooped the ice cream into the hole, creating an ice cream cone.

Solution 5-1

Al Capone's business card read that he was a used furniture dealer. When the man at the door saw the name on the card, he knew that somebody was aware of his business dealings and threatened to shoot.

Solution 5-2

The neighbors had no eyebrows. The time was ancient Egypt, and Egyptians would shave off their eyebrows if their cat died.

Solution 5-3

Armored knights used to lift their eyewear to identify themselves. This custom eventually led to the modern military salute.

Solution 5-4

In 1752, England and the American colonies adopted the new Gregorian calendar. They needed an eleven-day adjustment, so they dropped eleven days from the September calendar. The boy went to bed on September 3rd and the following day was September 14th.

Solution 5-5

Peter the Great, Tsar of Russia, admired European traditions and felt Russians needed to look and act more modern. He installed a beard tax and often had his officials stop men on the streets to cut off their beards. Since this man had forgotten to shave off his entire beard as the new tax was installed, he was pulled aside by an official and his beard was cut.

Solution 5-6

In April 1938, New York passed a law requiring syphilis tests for marriage license applicants. Charlotte and her fiancé were getting married within the month so she went to get the test. Her parents had not heard of the law and were surprised when she mentioned it.

Solution 5-7

In 1921, some Atlantic City

business owners created the Miss America competition as a "bathing beauty" contest to help extend the summer tourist season.

Solution 5-8

In 1986, Admiral Sir Henry Rawson ordered his fleet into Zanzibar waters so they could disembark to watch a cricket match. The Sultan of Zanzibar declared war against Britain because of the concentration of warships in his waters. He sent his lone battleship, and it was immediately destroyed. The war lasted just under 38 minutes and is the shortest war on record.

Solution 5-9

It is said that around 1500 B.C. in Egypt a woman's shaved head was often considered the ultimate in feminine beauty. Of course, even if they didn't think so, women in Egypt would shave their heads for other reasons. They were able to keep cool in the summer heat, hygiene was much easier,

and they liked to replace their natural hair with wigs.

Solution 5-10

In 1873, the Empress of Japan appeared in public wearing her natural eyebrows and unblackened teeth. Until that time, Japanese women traditionally shaved their eyebrows and blackened their teeth. Some say that they colored them black because the white powder they wore on their faces contrasted with their teeth and made them look yellow. Others say only savages and wild animals had long white teeth.

Solution 5-11

Richeborg, a dwarf who was only 23 inches tall as an adult, was a secret agent during the French Revolution. He was often disguised as an infant and carried through Paris, all while carrying secret dispatches and listening to those around him.

Solution 5-12

President James Garfield was

shot on July 2, 1881. He lay dying for two months because surgeons would not operate unless they knew the location of the bullet. Alexander Graham Bell visited the White House with his new invention, a magnetometer. He hoped to locate the bullet, but the results he received upon scanning the President's body were strange and inconclusive. What the physicians and Bell did not know was that Garfield was lying on a metal-spring mattress, also a new invention. Had they placed him on the floor to conduct the metal detector test, they would have likely found the bullet.

Solution 5-13

In 1763, British Captain Simon Ecuyer served in defending Fort Pitt against the Delaware Indians. He ordered blankets to be distributed to the Indians attacking the fort. Unbeknown to the Indians who received the "gifts," the blankets had been infested with the smallpox virus that had broken out among the refugees within the court. The Indians were ravaged by the smallpox epidemic, although it is unknown if the blankets were the sole source of infection.

Solution 5-14

The man was killed for drinking it. During the 1500s and 1600s in Turkey, drinking coffee was punishable by death.

Solution 5-15

Johnson wanted to be president of the United States, but denied the chance to run as vice president under Senator Knox because he did not want to be second on the ticket. He was later offered a chance to run as vice president for Warren Harding, the party nominee. Johnson again refused. Both men died within a few years, and had Johnson been vice president, he would have succeeded them and become president himself.

Solution 5-16

It was seventeenth-century England and he had paid admission to enter Bedlam, London's lunatic hospital. The hospital raised money by charging admission to see the inmates in cages.

Solution 5-17

He wore an earring. It is often said that a pirate wore a gold earring to carry his wealth around with him. Others say that pirates wore an earring to see more clearly (due to an acupressure point in the ear) or to offset an imbalance that helps with seasickness. Of course, there are also people who say that pirates wore earrings to be fashionable!

Solution 5-18

Rodrigo de Jerez is thought to be the first smoker outside of the Americas, having returned to Spain after a trip to Cuba. He had observed villagers inhaling smoke from tobacco leaves, and when he arrived home he brought the tobacco with him. When they saw the smoke coming out of his nose and mouth, holy inquisitors accused him of consorting with the devil and sentenced him to prison for seven years.

Solution 5-19

The castrati were boys who were castrated at a young age to preserve their high-pitched voice. They were then cast to sing female parts because it was immoral for women to sing and be onstage with men.

Solution 5-20

In 1977, Ruth van Herpen kissed a white monochrome canvas being displayed in an art museum. Her reason? She wanted to cheer it up because the work "looked so cold." It cost the museum $1,260 to remove her lipstick from the canvas.

Solution 5-21

During the Revolutionary War, a loyalist spy brought a message to the headquarters of the Hessian commander, Colonel Johann Rall in Trenton, New

Jersey. Rall was playing cards and refused to see the spy. The spy wrote his message on a slip of paper, which was taken to Rall. The colonel proceeded to put the paper in his pocket and left the note unread. Later that day General George Washington and his army launched a sneak attack on Trenton and won their first battle. Rall was found on the battlefield with the message still in his pocket

Solution 5-22

In 1628, the Swedish 64-gun warship, Vasa, capsized on its maiden voyage. It was less than one nautical mile away from shore. Vasa was greater than any ship built at that time, but the gun decks held 64 bronze cannons that allowed the boat to sink quickly after listing in a squall.

Solution 5-23

In the nineteenth century, craftsmen who made hats were often subjected to mercury poison from the solution used to treat the felt. They were known to be irrational, had uncontrollable muscle twitching, and could not think clearly. This later evolved into the familiar expression "mad as a hatter."

Solution 5-24

In World War I, German Pioneer-Sergeant Kunze was investigating Fort Douaumont in France when he stumbled upon a tunnel. He worked his way inside the fort, captured the artillery teams, and locked the remaining garrison using a steel door to a room where they were attending a training lecture.

Solution 5-25

In 1968, a Detroit house burglar committed a burglary and left his dog at the scene of the crime as he fled. The police arrived and told the dog to go home. They then followed the dog straight to the burglar's house.

Solution 5-26

In 1947, the destroyer HMS

Saintes accidentally missed its target, but hit the tugboat that was pulling the target through the water. The tugboat quickly sank.

Solution 5-27

In 1948, a man arrived at a bank in Japan and told the employees he was a doctor and was to inoculate the staff against dysentery. Instead, he gave them poison and robbed the bank while the employees were incapacitated. Sadamichi Hirasawa was later arrested for the crime, tried under military occupation, and sentenced to death by hanging. Hirasawa's attorneys argued that the Japanese constitution protects citizens from self-destruction, and hanging was a self-strangulation. Hirasawa went to prison instead and remained there for thirty years.

Solution 5-28

In 413 B.C., while at war with the Spartans, the Athenian army learned that the enemy soldiers at Syracuse had received more men and supplies. The Athenian army decided to pull the Athenian troops stationed there and bring them back to Athens. As they were about to depart, a lunar eclipse occurred. Viewed as a bad omen, Commander Nicias called off the departure. The Spartans arrived and defeated him and his forces.

Solution 5-29

William Henry Harrison was elected to be the president of the United States in 1840. His inauguration speech in March, 1841 was one of the longest on record. He was not wearing a jacket, developed a cold that later turned into pneumonia, and he died a month after taking office.

Solution 5-30

In the 1900 Olympics, the French marathon participants were accused of cheating. The Americans arrived at the finish line to find the French athletes already there and lounging. The Americans said that the French had never passed them, so they must have cheated (it was speculated that they used horses to run the course). Had the French gone a bit slower and given the appearance of having run the race, the accusations might have been contested.

Solution 5-31

In the Civil War, medical science was horrendous. Over half of the deaths during the war were not from battle; they were caused from infection and disease. These often spread in the hospitals because the physicians did not take precautionary measures. This man, wounded in battle, thought his chances of survival were better if he was not treated in a hospital.

Solution 5-32

In ancient Greece, athletes competed and exercised without any clothes on. In fact, the word gymnasium is a derivative of the word gymnos, which means "nude."

Solution 5-33

He knew that the police were at the door. It is said that in eighteenth-century European gambling dens, there was an employee designated to swallow the dice in the event of a police raid.

Solution 5-34

William Hewson, a friend of Benjamin Franklin, was an anatomist. He died young from blood poisoning after cutting himself while dissecting a putrid corpse.

Solution 5-35

In ancient China, patients only paid their doctors when they were well, not when they were sick. Everyone believed that it was the doctor's job to prevent a disease, so the patients were often paid by the doctor if they lost their health.

Solution 5-36

The teacher typically taught the order of the planets as My Very Eager Mother Just Served Us Nine Pizzas. But from 1979 through 1999, Pluto was inside the orbit of Neptune and he chose to rearrange the mnemonic device.

Solution 5-37

After the French Revolution, a merchant could be executed for selling sour wine. It was determined to be "against national interest."

Solution 5-38

It is said that Babe Ruth wore a cabbage leaf in his baseball cap to keep him cool. He changed the leaf every two innings.

Solution 5-39

The "employee" was a codetalker and was a soldier during World War II. These Navajo soldiers created and used a radio code based on their native language. The soldier who received the message had to decode a string of unrelated Navajo words that represented English letters. The code was the only one never broken by the enemy.

Solution 5-40

David Rice Atchison legally became the president of the United States for a twenty-four hour period, although he was not elected to office or sworn in. President-elect Zachary Taylor was scheduled to be sworn in on a Sunday, but he was religious and insisted on waiting until Monday. Under the law, the presidency fell to the vice president, who had already resigned, and then to the president pro tem of the Senate, who was David Rice Atchison.

Solution 5-41

He had paid to have his blood withdrawn. During the Middle Ages, and even later in some areas of the world, barbers cut hair, shaved beards, and also performed bloodletting procedures. This practice involved withdrawing a substantial amount of blood from a patient in the belief that it would assist in curing a disease or illness. The symbolic striped barber pole is derived from the process. The red represents the blood, the white portrays the tourniquet, and the pole represents the stick that the patient would hold in his hand to dilate his veins.

Solution 5-42

The platoon was crossing a bridge. Traditionally soldier-break step when walking across a bridge because the patterned steps would otherwise create a resonance oscillation. One such event caused the Maine at Angers bridge in France to break, sending 478 soldiers into the river and 226 of them to their deaths.

Solution 5-43

It was 1916 and the bricks were being used to build a bank in Vernal, Utah. The bricks were sent in fifty-pound packages via the postal service because it was cheaper than sending them freight.

Solution 5-44

Dieter Schepp was part of The Flying Wallendas' high-wire

act in 1962. The family created a seven-person pyramid and then walked along the high-wire in formation. Schepp reportedly lost his footing and fell to his death. Two family members fell—one died and one was paralyzed. The other family members were able to grab the wire and hold on until a net was brought in.

Solution 5-45

The green wallpaper that Betsy had helped pick out was a William Morris design. Unknown to customers at the time, the green shade was a compound made of arsenic and copper. In damp conditions the arsenic was converted into a poisonous vapor. It is said that Napoleon's house on St. Helena was decorated with the green wallpaper as well. Traces of arsenic were found in strands of his hair years after his death.

Solution 5-46

During the 1930s, coal miners in the town of Madrid, New

Mexico, created Christmas light displays that used 50,000 lights and hundreds of thousands of hours of coal-generated electricity. One airline changed its route to allow passengers to see the display from the sky.

Solution 5-47

Harry S Truman's middle name is S. The letter is not an abbreviation for a longer name, but instead was given to him by his parents as a compromise in naming him after various relatives whose names began with the letter "S."

Solution 5-48

With the beginning of the Civil War, residents of the northwestern counties of Virginia were against seceding, so they took matters into their own hands. They created their own state, which was to be a part of the Union.

Solution 5-49

During the fourteenth century, John Wycliffe translated the Bible into English so that average people could benefit from the Scriptures. He was brought to trial because church leaders believed it was dangerous for ordinary people to read the word of God without the benefit of the clergy. Wycliffe's Bibles were later forbidden, and the church condemned him, burning his body thirty-one years after his death.

Solution 5-50

Although it is often suggested that the $ sign is a U superimposed over an S, another explanation comes from a different location. The name of the dollar was used in imitation from the Spanish dollar, also known as pesos or piastres. The monetary amount was often written as ps, and when written quickly, it became a $. Florian Cajori documents this information, including both single and double stroke dollar signs, in his book on mathematical notations.

Solution 5-51

The Mason-Dixon line came about when Charles Mason and

Jeremiah Dixon were called in to survey the boundary between the feuding members of the colonies of Maryland and Pennsylvania. The original description of their boundaries did not match and George Calvert and William Penn took the matter to court. Ten years later they agreed on a compromise, and three years after that Mason and Dixon were recruited to survey the new border. The task took four years to complete.

Solution 5-52

In 1693, the postage rate to send a letter was based on the amount of light that could shine through the letter. The darker the light that shone through from the candle, the more expensive the postage rate would be.

Solution 5-53

The Great Fire of London in 1666 destroyed over 80 percent of the city, but only killed six people. Citizens were thankful because the fire saved thou-sands of lives by putting an end to the black plague, halt-ing the spread of the disease.

Solution 5-54

In 1949, Jack Wurm walked along a San Francisco beach and stumbled across a bottle with a piece of paper inside. He broke the bottle and found a paper inside, the last will and testament of Daisy Singer Alexander, the heiress to the Singer fortune. The note said that the finder of the bottle would inherit her estate, to be shared with her attorney. The courts accepted the document, which had been thrown in the water from London twelve years earlier. Wurm inherited over six million dollars in cash and Singer stock.

Solution 5-55

When Samuel Clemens (bet-ter known as Mark Twain) was born on November 30, 1835, Halley's comet was visible in the sky. He later said he would see the comet again before he died. On April 20, 1910, the comet passed overhead and Clemens passed away the following day.

Solution 5-56

In 1885 James Fraser Gluck, a benefactor of the Erie County Public Library, asked Mark Twain if he would be willing to send in a manuscript for preservation. The manuscript that he sent was The Adventures of Huckleberry Finn. Years later the library only had the second half of the manuscript available, and it was assumed that the first half was lost. As time progressed, proofreaders and typists mangled the first half of the book, since there was no original manuscript to review. In 1990, the first half was finally found in a trunk that once belonged to Gluck. It is assumed he took it home to review and never returned it.

Solution 5-57

During the tenth century, Abdul Kassem Ismael, the Grand Vizer of Persia, carried his library with him. He was an avid reader and he brought over 117,000 volumes. They were carried on 400 camels, which were taught to walk in a specific order to keep the works alphabetized.

Solution 5-58

In the seventh century, Queen Bathilde ended slavery in Western Europe after her husband died. She had been born into slavery and was sold to Clovis II, King of the Franks. He fell in love with Bathilde and married her. She became regent for their three young sons after the king died, and was able to outlaw slavery.

Solution 5-59

In 1887, Susanna M. Salter was the first woman elected as a United States mayor. Her name was entered on the ticket at the last minute by a group of men who believed women should have nothing to do with politics. Mrs. Salter was a member of a Woman's Christian Temperance Union, and so they added her name to the list of candidates in the hopes of embarrassing her. When the chairman of the Republican Party saw her name on the list, a delegation was sent to ask her if she would accept the position if she won. Mrs. Salter agreed and the delegation campaigned to local voters throughout the day, winning her two-thirds of the vote.

Solution 5-60

The man was the defendant. Valdamair Morelos confessed to murdering a judge in 1994 and told the judge that he wanted the death penalty. Unfortunately for him, California law requires a trial, in capital cases. At the trial Morelos assisted the prosecution, adding information to their descriptions, including admitting to blindfolding the victim.

Solution 6-1

The woman vacationed in La Paz, Bolivia. La Paz is 11,900 feet above sea level, and many people become sick due to the altitude.

Solution 6-2

In Siena, Italy, it is illegal to work as a prostitute if your name is Mary.

Solution 6-3

The woman was standing in the Four Corners (Arizona, Colorado, Utah, and New Mexico) with her feet in two of the states and her hands in the other two.

Solution 6-4

One, if you kept driving in circles.

Solution 6-5

250, if you kept driving back and forth across the same border, only going one mile into the state before turning around and coming back.

Solution 6-6

There are no rivers in Saudi Arabia, so he knew after days of traveling that he was in that country.

Solution 6-7

In Switzerland, the law requires that all citizens have a bomb shelter, or access to a bomb shelter, so she altered her estate plans to include one.

Solution 6-8

In the Malaysian state of Kuala Lumpur, local authorities are offering a cash payment for each photograph taken of people littering. The state has a horrible trash problem, and they are looking for ways to raise the level of cleanliness.

Solution 6-9

In Japan, a horizontal traffic light has red on the right instead of on the left. The man was color-blind, so when the light turned, he could only see the brightness change, not the color displayed. He thought it was green, drove forward into oncoming traffic, and caused a traffic accident.

Solution 6-10

People from Michigan often describe the location of various cities in the Lower Peninsula by using their hand as the shape of the state. His mother told him that she gave birth to him in Lansing and pointed to the

palm of her hand to demonstrate where the city was.

Solution 6-11

In Providence, Rhode Island, it is against the law to jump off a bridge. She was given a citation.

Solution 6-12

Manuela was pregnant and wanted her son to be an American citizen. When she went into labor, she crossed the border and was pulled over by the border patrol. Her baby was born in the patrol car an hour later. Since he was born on Texan soil, he was considered a United States citizen.

Solution 6-13

He got his wife a cup of coffee every morning. In Saudi Arabia, a woman can get a divorce if her husband doesn't give her coffee.

Solution 6-14

The family lived in a small town in South America and found the burnt doll in a field. They had seen what they thought was a fireball fall from the sky and they thought the doll was a dead alien.

Solution 6-15

A road in a Delaware park separated the winter sleeping grounds from the spring breeding grounds for many local amphibians. The road was closed after spring-like conditions to allow the frogs, salamanders, and spring peepers to cross the road safely to mate.

Solution 6-16

A council of chaste villages told the couple, living in India, that their marriage was unacceptable because of the relationship between their villages. They were told that the sin could be undone if they accepted each other as siblings.

Solution 6-17

Colorado troopers are enforcing the "Left Lane Law," which requires using the left lane only as a passing lane. Ralph was dawdling in the left lane, so he was pulled over and given a ticket.

Solution 6-18

He lived in central China and his father was denied permission to give him the name "@." Since the name did not translate into Mandarin, as the law requires, he was given a more normal name.

Solution 6-19

They traveled to Honolulu to visit the Iolani Palace, the only royal residence on American soil.

Solution 6-20

They were riding in a gondola in Venice. At one point all gondolas were required to be painted black unless it was a special boat for a dignitary.

Solution 6-21

On a clear day you can see five states when you're on top of the Empire State Building in New York City. You can see New York, New Jersey, Connecticut, Massachusetts, and Pennsylvania.

Solution 6-22

He was talking on a cellular

phone while driving in Ireland, where it is illegal to do both activities at the same time. It is illegal in many other countries as well.

Solution 6-23

She separated from her husband and filed for a divorce later that year. While separated she became pregnant by another man, but under Washington law a husband is presumed the father of any child born within 300 days of a divorce. The judge for her case denied the divorce until paternity tests could be performed on the baby.

Solution 6-24

He carried a tessen, an iron fan. Tessen were popular concealed weapons in Japan because they were strong enough to deflect sword attacks, but could also be used as weapons, with their sharp metal ribs. It allowed ninjas to carry a weapon when they were in disguise.

Solution 6-25

Kerri was telling the truth. She visited Panama with her parents, and it's the only location where you can see the sun rise on the Pacific Ocean and set on the Atlantic. There is a bend in the isthmus where this phenomenon occurs.

Solution 6-26

They traveled on horses and brought along well-watered camels as pack animals. At periodic intervals they slaughtered the camels, removed the stomach full of water, and fed that water to the horses.

Solution 6-27

The trees were sacred, and the marriage was an effort to ward off an evil spell. The residents thought an evil eye had been cast on them, and nearly 1,000 people attended the wedding.

Solution 6-28

Since 1620 in Castrillo de Murcia, Spain, the town has celebrated the Catholic festival of Corpus Christi. Among the events that occur is a Baby-Jumping Colacho Festival. Adult men dress up as the devil and jump over infants to take all their evil with them, leaving the babies cleansed.

Solution 6-29

He flew into Portland on an extremely foggy day. The airport is equipped with an instrument runway, permitting the landing of an aircraft under restricted visibility.

Solution 6-30

In Fort Wayne, Indiana, the open-container law banned all open containers, not just those containing alcohol. Tom was pulled over for driving over the speed limit, and he began to yell at the police officer. The officer would typically have ignored the open bag of potato chips, but since Tom was aggravating him, he wrote out a ticket for $50.

Solution 6-31

In 1999, the Canadian Cabinet began to allow the use of iron oxide (rust) as a coloring agent for the skins of Black Forest ham. A meat processing company had requested the change, stating that rust was less expensive and easier to use than the traditional caramel. They also said the additive was safe for human consumption.

Solution 6-32

In the eighteenth century, German university students often took part in saber duels. When they were injured, they preferred that their faces remained scarred as a reference to their social standing and their ability to duel.

Solution 6-33

A whale skeleton, complete and well preserved, was found in the Egyptian desert. Many have been found in a sandstone formation that represents an ancient seabed.

Solution 6-34

The golfer was playing with friends at the Port Royal Plantation golf course in South Carolina when he hit a ball that bounced onto an alligator's back and remained there. The golfer decided to drop a new ball, and according to course rules, was not penalized a stroke.

Solution 6-35

In India, Sari weavers purchase condoms by the thousands to use on their thread spools as a lubricant, or to polish the gold and silver threads on the garments.

Solution 6-36

Erin started off in Alaska and stayed there. Alaska is the most northern, most eastern, and most western of the states in the United States. Although on a map it does not appear to be the most eastern state, the Aleutian Islands stretch across the 180° line of Longitude, into the Eastern Hemisphere.

Solution 6-37

The tourist was in Vietnam and the shop owner handed him coins. The Vietnamese use the dong, which is a paper currency. No coins are used.

Solution 6-38

The ancient Egyptians thought that onions kept evil spirits away. In keeping with those assumptions, they often swore an oath with one hand on an onion. When the man's neighbor would not hold the onion to make his oath, the first man became upset, assumed the other man was lying, and negated their agreement.

Solution 6-39

According to the law in Providence, Rhode Island, no store is allowed to sell a toothbrush on the Sabbath.

Solution 6-40

In North Dakota it is legal to shoot an Indian on horseback from a covered wagon. In the parade, George was riding on a covered wagon float, and he shot his ex-friend, a Native American, who was riding on horseback.

Solution 6-41

Fearful of the deadly Marburg virus that had already killed over 200 people in a northern Angolan town, citizens gave up their traditional greeting of hugs for tapping right legs. The virus was being spread through contact with bodily fluids, so they avoided skin contact and instead would touch one another with clothed parts of their body.

Solution 6-42

The Pekingese dog was once considered sacred among Chinese royalty, and were bred and carefully guarded in the Imperial Palace. They were often given their own private palaces with servants, guards, and wet nurses.

Solution 6-43

Officials with the Ohio Department of Transportation are considering reversing the flow of traffic on a stretch of highway in the hope of reducing congestion. Although this would force drivers onto the left side of the street, it would allow traffic in both directions from Route 224 to Interstate 75 to move continuously.

Solution 6-44

The flag is on the moon.

Solution 6-45

Samuel waited for the tide to come in. In the upper basins of the Bay of Fundy in Canada, the peak vertical tidal range is approximately 50 feet. As the tide came in, he floated up to the top of the cliff and stepped onto it.

Solution 6-46

They live on islands.

Solution 6-47

They live within 50 miles of their birthplace.

Solution 6-48

The real estate agent mentioned she knew of a way to purchase property on the Bay of Rainbows (Sinus Iridum) on the moon. Jennifer was more interested in purchasing property she could live in today.

Solution 6-49
They went to the town of Santa Claus, Indiana.

Solution 6-50
Craig lived in Philadelphia. The gentleman behind him asked for a "Philly cheesesteak," but citizens of the city just call them "cheesesteaks."

Solution 6-51
Katherine was driving into Pennsylvania, which was the first of the fifty United States to list their website URL on a license plate. On the website Katherine could find visitor information, among other useful tips for residents.

Solution 6-52
She lived in Kentucky. Officially Pennsylvania, Kentucky, Virginia, and Massachusetts are all commonwealths.

Solution 6-53
Shirley lived along an earthquake fault line in California. She had read research discussing animal behavior prior to earthquakes and remembered her pets acting strangely before a large earthquake a couple of years ago. When they began acting oddly, she decided to visit her parents in Nevada for a few days in case another earthquake occurred.

Solution 6-54
John was visiting his brother in Bolivia, which has two capital cities. John went to Sucre, but his brother was in La Paz.

Solution 6-55
She was in Antarctica, which is considered a desert because it receives less than 10 inches of rain annually.

Solution 6-56
Jennifer lived in Hammerfest, Norway, where the sun shines twenty-four hours a day for part of the year. Many of the local inhabitants work through the night in preparation for winter and its days of complete darkness.

Solution 6-57

In May of 1981, small green frogs rained down on the city of Naphlion. The Greek Meteorological Institute gathered that they were picked up by a strong wind and carried all the way from North Africa.

Solution 6-58

The hotel is an ice igloo created for only four months during the winter in Norway. The Alta Igloo Hotel offers beds, lounges, an ice chapel, and more. They offer comfortable mattresses and sleeping bags to keep you warm during the chilly nights.

Solution 6-59

She was at the Dead Sea, where ultraviolet rays are filtered through the thick atmosphere and an evaporation layer. The sunlight rays there are high in UVA rays, and low in UVB.

Solution 7-1

A recent urban legend stated that drinking Mountain Dew could be used as a contraceptive because its high caffeine volume worked to lower the sperm count in males.

Solution 7-2

The woman was driving while alcohol-impaired. She saw the lights of a police car behind her as he signaled for her to pull over and she panicked. She had heard that sucking on a copper penny causes a breathalyzer to register negative blood alcohol. Unfortunately for her, it is an urban legend.

Solution 7-3

The man had climbed a transmission tower and decided he didn't want to climb back down when he had to urinate. He peed near the wire, the power arched up his urine stream, and blew him right off the tower.

Solution 7-4

Urban legend has it that in the early 1900s a construction worker was helping to build a bridge. One day he lost his footing on the rigging and fell into concrete that had recently been poured to create the pillars of the bridge. The construction company knew that he would not survive, and did not want to destroy the bridge, so they paid the worker's wife a good deal of money to keep his body buried there.

Solution 7-5

The woman was coming home from dropping off her dog at the veterinarian. Earlier that day she had arrived home from work to find her dog lying on the ground gasping for air. She took him to the veterinarian, who had to perform a tracheotomy and told the woman to go home during the procedure. As the vet did the surgery, he found three fingers lodged in the dog's throat. He immediately called the woman to warn her that there might be an intruder in her house.

Solution 7-6

He put on a security guard uniform, placed an "out of order" sign on the bank's night deposit box, and proceeded to collect all of the deposits from bank customers.

Solution 7-7

The woman was contemplating taking her own life and as a last resort she asked God for a sign not to go through with it. The phone immediately started ringing. When she looked at the Caller ID, it said "Almighty God" and she was so startled that she couldn't pick up the phone. She decided against committing suicide. What she did not know was that the pastor from the Almighty God church had been calling his wife and had misdialed his home phone number.

Solution 7-8

The bus driver was transporting twenty mental patients when he stopped to get a couple of drinks at a local bar. When he walked back out to the bus, he noticed that the patients had all escaped. He needed a solution, so he stopped at a bus stop and told the first twenty people that he would transport them for free. When he arrived at the asylum he told the employees there that the "patients" on board his bus were very excitable and told fabulous lies.

Solution 7-9

Before her husband died, he had a telephone installed in his crypt in case he was accidentally entombed. He died, was placed in the crypt, and a few days later neighbors found his wife, dead on the floor of a heart attack, holding the phone. After her funeral, when they opened the crypt to bury her body alongside her husband's, they found the phone inside was off the hook.

Solution 7-10

She was afraid when she saw a man in the shadows. She put the car in reverse and backed up quickly, but stopped after only 10 feet. She slammed on the gas again and heard a scream. She quickly got out of the car, to find her boyfriend

hanging from the tree. One end of the rope had been tied to her car, the rope was draped over a limb on the tree and her boyfriend was tied to the other end. As she drove away she ran over him and then hung him as the rope lost its slack.

Solution 7-11

This puzzle is based on the urban legend of Ronald Opus. His father often waved an unloaded gun around in arguments with his mother, but one day Ronald loaded the gun in the hopes that his father would shoot his mother and Ronald could inherit the family money. An hour after loading the gun, he chose to commit suicide by jumping off the building that his parents lived in. At the moment he jumped, his father was shouting at his mother and pulled the trigger. The bullet missed her, blew out the glass window, and hit Ronald directly in the head as he fell past. Ronald landed in a safety net placed below by construction workers, but was dead from the bullet wound.

Solution 7-12

Earlier in the day two women exited a department store and found a dead cat in the parking lot. Being a cat-lover, Jane placed the items she had purchased in her friend's bag, and then put the cat in her bag, covered with tissue. They placed their bags in the car with the intent of walking to a nearby restaurant for lunch. Jane decided to keep the bag containing the cat on the roof of the trunk so that the smell would not permeate their newly purchased items. As they were eating lunch, Jane saw a woman sneak past the car and snatch the bag. The thief entered the restaurant, opened the bag, gasped, and fell to the ground in a faint.

Solution 7-13

She kept the lights off so as not to disturb her roommate. The following morning, when she arrived, she saw police officers outside. They allowed her in the room, and there, scrawled on the wall in blood, were the words "Aren't you glad you didn't turn the light on?"

Solution 7-14

"Thaw the chicken."

Solution 7-15

She and her husband were staying in Mexico and one morning she found an odd-looking, small dog outside her room. She fed it, and allowed the dog to sleep in their bed that night. She fell in love and decided to take him back home with her. While on the bus to the airport, she asked one of the locals if he knew the breed of dog she was taking home. He told her that it was not a dog, it was a large Mexican rat!

Solution 7-16

After the girl pumped gas and went to step into her car, the gas station attendant yelled at her to come inside because she hadn't paid. She furiously turned around and went in to argue with him, but he apologized and told her to stay inside. He had seen a man climb into the backseat of her car while she was pumping gas, and had just needed a way to keep her out of the car. They called the police and the man was apprehended.

Solution 7-17

The rabbit had died and George buried it in the backyard. The next day his neighbor's dog dug up the rabbit and brought it home. The neighbor felt terrible, thinking his dog had killed it. Since there were no teeth marks or visible signs of death, he shampooed the rabbit, blow dried the hair, and put it back in its cage. Later that day George arrived home to find the clean rabbit, still dead, back in its home.

Solution 7-18

There's an urban legend that a man had his wife's body encased in a glass coffee table that he kept in his living room. He couldn't stand to be with-out her and he wanted her to be with him always.

Solution 7-19

The Egyptians were hungry and dug into the honey. One man complained that he found a hair. Others discovered more hairs, and finally they pulled out a child's body from the honey. It had been buried there centuries ago. The entire group became extremely sick to their stomachs and a few vomited on the ground.

Solution 7-20

The family often received packages from their overseas relatives. One day a package arrived with the jar in it, but no note. Since they often received food items, they assumed it was a drink mix and drank it. A week later they received a note saying that their great uncle had died and they had placed his ashes in the jar because he wanted his ashes spread around his hometown.

Solution 7-21

A teenager bought a new brand of shrink-to-fit jeans and decided that the perfect fit could be achieved by wearing them in the bath. The jeans became so tight that she died of suffocation.

Solution 7-22

Urban legends say that there was a babysitter who took drugs and accidentally put the baby in the oven, mistaking it for a turkey. In this instance, the parents immediately went home because she told them she was cooking a turkey, but they knew that there were no turkeys in the house.

Solution 7-23

After the friends could not find him, employees at the golf course began to suspect that a crocodile had emerged from the lake and eaten him. They got permission to dissect the crocodile, and in the remains of the stomach they found the golfer's arm and other body parts.

Solution 7-24

The tug-of-war contest took place in Taipei and included over 1,600 participants. The rope broke and the rebounding force snapped off the arms of two men.

Solution 7-25

The teenager was pretending to hang himself as the guests drove by on a hayride. On October 29th the stunt went bad and the noose tightened, causing him to die.

Solution 7-26

On August 21, 1986, on Lake Nyos in Cameroon, the lake "turned over," causing the bottom layer to shoot to the surface and deposit over 100 million cubic meters of carbon dioxide to sweep over the valley surrounding it. The gas suffocated the inhabitants immediately, causing 1,746 deaths.

Solution 7-27

He was recharging his cell phone when it started to ring. He answered the phone while it was still attached to the wall. A current went through the phone and into his body, throwing him to the ground. He died shortly thereafter.

Solution 7-28

Josh had a habit of putting the tee in his mouth after driving the ball, and reusing it on the next ball. Throughout the course of the day, he had ingested a lethal dose of pesticide that the golf course sprayed on the grass.

Solution 7-29

The woman had a nightmare the night before that contained a hearse driver who drove up to her house and said, "There's room for one more." The next day she was shopping and was about to get on the elevator to return to the ground floor. The elevator was rather crowded and, as she neared the entrance, the operator turned to her and said, "There's room for one more." The face was the same as in her nightmare, and she quickly stepped away. The elevator closed, the cables broke, and everyone in the elevator died.

Solution 7-30

The doctor examined the mother and she had the plague. The hotel and city officials did not want to lose the local tourism by disclosing the information, so they removed all traces of the mother while the daughter was gone.

Solution 7-31

The woman had lost her job, her husband, and her most important possessions. She was desperate and decided to take her life. The only problem was that, due to nonpayment, the gas company shut off her gas hours before she attempted suicide.

Solution 7-32

The babysitter was late to arrive and called to say she would be there in 10 minutes. The parents had to catch an airplane, so they left the baby in the highchair with some snacks and a toy. They left the back door open for the babysitter but it blew closed in the wind shortly after they left. The babysitter arrived to find that the doors were locked and assumed the parents had taken the baby. A week later when the parents arrived home, the baby was still strapped in the chair.

Solution 7-33

A large nail stuck out of the floor of her parent's bedroom floor. They told her never to touch it, but one day when they were away she decided to see once and for all what the nail did. She pulled it out and 10 minutes later the downstairs neighbor was knocking on her door. When she opened the door he was covered in shards of glass and had blood seeping from many scratches. Apparently the nail was holding up the glass chandelier in his living room.

Solution 7-34

His wife had written him earlier in the week, desperate because she needed help plowing the

fields to plant crops on the family farm. Her husband sent the letter because he knew that the police would arrive and dig up the soil to look for the money and drugs. They spent all day looking and never found anything, but the fields were now ready for planting.

Solution 7-35

In 1989, a financial analyst purchased a picture from a flea market for $4 because he liked the frame. When he went to deconstruct the frame to remove the picture, an original copy of the Declaration of Independence fell out from between the canvas and the backing. He later received $2.42 million for the document in an auction.

Solution 7-36

In April 1995, a man committed suicide because he thought his half share of a five-week ticket on Britain's National Lottery had expired. He believed that he would have been a multi-millionaire, but had he actually held a valid ticket, it wouldn't have been worth much because he only had four of the six numbers correct.

Solution 7-37

They had taken a rock from a Hawaii beach and had had very bad luck and medical problems since they returned to their home. They packaged up the rock with a note to return the rock to the beach and sent it to the hotel in which they had previously stayed.

Solution 7-38

In 1999, David Phillips purchased over 12,150 cups of Healthy Choice chocolate pudding in order to get 1.25 million free frequent flyer miles through a promotion the company was having. He needed to purchase the individual servings in order to get the bar code on the product.

Solution 7-39

In 1929, a woman murdered her husband over his bidding and playing of a hand of bridge they were playing with a couple of friends. She called him a name, he retaliated by grabbing her arm, and the argument escalated until she went to get a gun from her mother's room and shot him.

Solution 7-40

Carrie walked out to her car and a woman stepped out with a bottle of designer perfume that she said she was selling at a 75 percent discount. The woman offered to let Carrie smell the perfume, and Carrie did, only to black out from the fumes. She awoke to find her car missing, along with the cash in her wallet.

Solution 7-41

Joseph opened an envelope and placed some cash inside that he wanted to deposit. He licked the envelope, but the glue had been laced with cyanide and caused his death.

Solution 7-42

The boy's grandfather was

a rancher, and one day he stomped on the head of a rattlesnake after shooting it. Days later, he died. When his son was older, he took the boots and wore them, also dying days later. When the grandson inherited the boots, he learned of the deaths and inspected the boot, only to find a fang imbedded in the heel.

Solution 7-43
Carter walked out with a wheelbarrow full of straw every evening at the end of his shift. The security guard was suspicious, looked through the straw, but never found anything. When Carter retired, the security guard said that he knew Carter was stealing something, what was it? Carter replied, "I was stealing wheelbarrows."

Solution 7-44
The daughter went to the party and then left with her boyfriend, who was drunk. He was driving when he hit another vehicle head on. The couple inside the second vehicle died instantly, along with her boyfriend. The daughter ended up in the hospital, where she woke only long enough to tell the nurse to tell her parents she loved them. The nurse didn't have the heart to tell her that her parents had been in the other car, looking for her.

Solution 7-45
The man ran off with his new girlfriend, sending his wife a letter requesting that she sell his luxury car and send him half the money. In an act of spite, she sold the car for $20 and sent him a check for $10.

Solution 7-46
A group of students was late for a test. They told the teacher that they had had a flat tire and couldn't make it in time. He gave them a make-up exam and when they opened the test they had one question: "Which tire was it?"

Solution 7-47
The student was in a college fraternity and copied a paper that had been used years

ago. The professor had actually written that exact paper. Instead of failing the student, he gave him an A and wrote "When I wrote this, I only got a C. I thought it deserved an A."

Solution 7-48

She took a stake to put in the ground to prove that she had been there. The next morning she still hadn't arrived home, and when the girls went to look for her, they found her at the grave. She had accidentally placed the stake through her nightgown and died of fright trying to get away from the grave.

Solution 7-49

Janet decided to dry her hair in the microwave. She falsely locked the door with a knife and placed her head inside the unit. When she was found and taken to the hospital, her death was ruled as "boiled brains."

Solution 7-50

Urban legend has it that the gun was shot from someone on top of a hill. The bullet initially passed through a man's scrotum before embedding itself in the woman's ovary, impregnating her. Although she was telling the truth when she told her husband she had not slept with any other men, he did not believe her and asked for a divorce.

Solution 7-51

The plumber fixed the clogged pipes and told the man not to throw his condoms in the toilet because it blocked the drains. The man confronted his wife when she got home, as he never used condoms when they made love. She was upset and confessed to having an affair.

Solution 7-52

Katherine had a friend call her boyfriend at work to say that his business card had been pulled from a bowl at a local business and he was going to receive a fresh bouquet. The friend then asked where the flowers should be sent. If the boyfriend said Katherine, she knew everything was fine. If he said somebody else, she could quickly leave the relationship.

Solution 7-53

The survey was for an airline company promotion that she had supposedly accepted with her husband. It had been given out to men with a good amount of frequent flyer miles, and was a "companion ticket" for their wives. Unfortunately, Laura had not been the recipient of the companion ticket. It had gone to her husband's lover. He confessed to having an affair.

Solution 7-54

It was right after midnight and Anne had gone into the bathroom to stare at the mirror and chant "Bloody Mary" twelve times like they had discussed in their ghost stories. Although nothing appeared in the mirror, she was frightened from the expectations of what she would see.

Solution 7-55

She had received an e-mail saying that some bananas from Costa Rica had been infected with necrotizing fasciitis, a flesh-eating virus. She was concerned and asked for the bread back from all but one of her friends. The friend that Martha didn't call was one she suspected was having an affair with her husband.

Solution 7-56

She took her son to the local fast food chain. After eating a kid's meal, he wanted to go play in the jungle gym area outside. He played in the ball pit for ten minutes, but when he came out he was rubbing his arm and kept saying he was hurt. After they went home the mother noticed red welts on his legs and within a couple of hours he was dead. She found out later that the fast food restaurant had found baby rattlesnakes buried at the bottom of the pit.

Solution 7-57

The man knew of three questions to ask someone to determine if they were suffering from a stroke. 1) Ask the individual to smile. 2) Ask her to raise her arms. 3) Ask her to speak a short sentence. These three tasks encompass the range of symptoms that occur with a stroke.

Solution 7-58

In 1873, a British mill engineer hired clerks to study the roulette tables at the Beaux-Arts Monte Carlo Casino. One of the wheels was biased and the engineer won a good deal of money after he calculated which numbers the ball fell on most often. The casino tried moving the wheels around, but the engineer recognized a scratch on the wheel and continued to win more money. The casino finally had a set of movable frets created by a Parisian manufacturer. They won some money back, but the engineer quit while he was ahead.

Solution 8-1

The building was a library and the engineers failed to include the additional weight of all the books. This is based on the Main Library at Indiana University, where the library continues to sink each year.

Solution 8-2

He ran a lighthouse, and when the room went dark he knew that some of the ships would crash.

Solution 8-3

The down pillows that he received cost much more than the previous shipment. When he called the manufacturer, he was told, "the price of down is up."

Solution 8-4

He was having an instant message (IM) conversation on the computer, and he saved the file to his hard drive.

Solution 8-5

He flew on the Concorde from London to New York City. Flying through the time zones and the speed of the airplane got him to New York City two hours before he left.

Solution 8-6
He had vanity license plates on his car that read "IMLWYER."

Solution 8-7
It was St. Patrick's Day and she forgot to wear green to the office. He was Irish and a big fan of the holiday, so he pinched all of the employees who hadn't worn green.

Solution 8-8
The house was of a recently deceased colleague. The officer fainted when he saw a figure in the house and thought it to be a ghost. It was actually a thief, and he carried the belongings out the back door without disturbing the police officer where he lay on the porch.

Solution 8-9
It was International Women's Day and Russian police stopped women drivers to hand out flowers instead of speeding tickets.

Solution 8-10
Trent was flying an airplane and was forced to circle for more than half an hour after the air traffic controller dozed off.

Solution 8-11
Cindy was applying to go to an Ivy League university. She learned of a way to hack into an Internet site to see the results of her application for admission before the official notification. The school was able to determine which students checked the website, and rejected all of the applications.

Solution 8-12
He was a professional boxer, and after fighting in a boxing match, the judges made their decision for his opponent. He retired from the sport the following day, ending his career as a boxer.

Solution 8-13
A public broadcasting station was conducting a test on the emergency natural disaster area of their Web site. After the

tests were finished, the system was not shut down, allowing the information to be accessed by outside users for over a day.

Solution 8-14

Officials had sent subpoenas to anyone contacted by the defendant while he was in jail. He had written his dog, Carter, and that got the puppy on the witness list. Unfortunately, dogs were not allowed in the courthouse.

Solution 8-15

One day they found many beached dolphins in the Florida Keys. They surmised that a loud burst of sonar had frightened them, causing them to quickly surface and experience sudden decompression.

Solution 8-16

The burglar was wearing a Halloween mask depicting the President of the United States. The clerk was laughing so hard that the burglar turned and walked out.

Solution 8-17

Catherine was elderly and living in an extended-care facility. Her roommate died quietly and when the ambulance driver came he forgot to check the wristbands to make sure he had the right person. Catherine was a sound sleeper and awoke in the morgue later that night.

Solution 8-18

He was a blind doctor.

Solution 8-19

He was a co-founder of the company and had a significant stake in the stock. He cut his own salary down to $1 and cashed out a portion of the stock to live on.

Solution 8-20

The thief had failed to cut eyeholes in the pillowcase and had to lift it up to see where the exit was located. One of the customers in the store recognized his face.

Solution 8-21

The guard was attending to

the back of the truck when the driver slammed on his brakes to avoid running a red light. A load of boxed coins fell on the guard's head and crushed him.

Solution 8-22
The librarian was the student's father. He knew that his daughter had no cash on her, so he paid the fine himself.

Solution 8-23
Ralph did not know that it was a common courtesy to tip the skycaps working outside the airport. Whenever he flew on the second airline, the skycaps purposely rerouted his luggage to a different destination as a way to get back at him.

Solution 8-24
She was a freelance writer and often submitted work to a national newspaper. She wrote a piece on the hunt, even though it had been postponed for a few days due to bad weather. She fabricated gruesome details and stories about the hunt, and the newspaper printed the story

without verifying any of the information.

Solution 8-25
The farmer's goat wandered through and ate the basket, along with the paper bills contained inside.

Solution 8-26
Unbeknown to him, Joshua's wife had a day job as a stripper. His friends threw him a surprise birthday party and his wife arrived in the birthday cake. They were both surprised when she jumped out without her top on.

Solution 8-27
The school had hosted a "stay in school" campaign and gave out pencils reading "too cool to drop out." The teacher had sharpened his down to read "cool to drop out," and now the phrase read, "drop out."

Solution 8-28
The employee worked for a printing plant that makes paper currency. He took home sheets of $20 bills that were flawed

and marked for destruction to spend on his own.

Solution 8-29
The man shot his tooth with a pistol to dislodge it and in the process blew a hole in his jaw. He had to go to the emergency room to have it repaired.

Solution 8-30
In this true story, the woman was a visiting scientist to a laboratory working on a vaccine for meningococcal disease. She later contracted the disease and developed blood poisoning. She had to have both legs and an arm amputated.

Solution 8-31
They jumped in a rowboat but did not know how to row. They were quickly captured as their feeble attempts at paddling kept them going in circles.

Solution 8-32
They were flying a space shuttle and could not make out any traditional landmarks on the ground far below.

Solution 8-33
He was an employee of the airport and worked to load luggage onto the airplanes. He was stowing a wheelchair when another employee closed the cargo door. The cargo area was heated and pressurized, so he was relatively comfortable for the flight.

Solution 8-34
The artist had created an image for an exhibit that depicted the United States president in an unfriendly light. The government wanted to know if he was consorting with terrorists or planning an assassination attempt.

Solution 8-35
He wrote the note on the stub of his paycheck, which also contained his name and address.

Solution 8-36
The thief helped himself to a glass of wine and a light snack while moving the items to his car. He decided to take a quick

catnap before leaving with the stolen goods, but the owner arrived home and called the police to arrest him.

Solution 8-37

The doctor told his patient that he needed more iron in his diet, so he went to the hardware store and purchased a bag of nails. After dinner that evening, he swallowed the nails and later went to the hospital in agony.

Solution 8-38

He slipped on the floor and collided with another chef who happened to be standing over a large kettle of black bean soup. The second chef fell into the kettle and died from the burns. The restaurant was closed to investigate the death.

Solution 8-39

The elderly man within the car had received a medical treatment that left traces of radioactivity within his body. The level was high enough to register on the nuclear alert, causing the fire department to take notice.

Solution 8-40

He determined that arsenic poisoning leaves traces of the chemical in almost all parts of the body, not just the stomach or liver. He could test the bones or hair of a murder victim and detect the arsenic long after death.

Solution 8-41

She was an astronaut. When she flew in space, in a zero gravity environment, her spine lengthened up to two inches due to the vertebrae stretching.

Solution 8-42

Thomas Jefferson wrote his epitaph and purposely left out that he had been president, possibly because he was dissatisfied with his actions during office. The epitaph reads, "Here was buried/Thomas Jefferson/Author of the Declaration of American Independence/of the Statute of Virginia for Religious Freedom/& Father of the University of Virginia."

Solution 8-43

Myra Bradwell passed the bar in 1869, but the state of Illinois would not allow her to practice law because she was married. At that time women were required to be available to their husbands at all times. Bradwell appealed the decision, ultimately taking it to the United States Supreme Court. In 1872 the law was overturned, but Bradwell did not obtain her license until 1892.

Solution 8-44

He sprayed pesticide on the plants to help them survive the winter. When the butterflies were released into the garden, they died from exposure to the chemicals.

Solution 8-45

He gave the teller the note through the drive-through pneumatic tube system. When the teller ignored him and did not send back any money through the tube, the thief waved his gun and left before the police could arrive.

Solution 8-46

Before departing from the moon, Alan Shepard hit three golf balls on the lunar surface. The first ball he buried in the dirt, the second rolled a short way before stopping, and the third drive was successful. Shepard had fashioned a six iron out of a sampling instrument before hitting the balls in his bulky space suit.

Solution 8-47

They were bouncing a message off the Moon. The U.S. Navy sent a transcontinental message from Washington D.C. to Wahiawa, Hawaii, in the mid 1950s as part of the Communication Moon Relay project.

Solution 8-48

He was video taping a Norwegian landscape using an infrared camera. He noticed a small moving object at eye level but thought nothing of it due to the size. Moments later, he was attacked by a polar bear. The polar bear has fur that is very well insulated and is very diffi-cult to detect by infrared cam-era. The nose does radiate heat, and that is the object that the photographer got a glimpse of.

Solution 8-49

In the 1930s hormone rese-arch was expanding. Scientists would take a sample of urine from an adult female, condense it, and inject it into a mouse (or even a rabbit, toad, or rat). After two or three days the laboratory would kill the mouse and exam-ine its ovaries. If the ovaries were swollen, it was deemed that the woman was pregnant. Many women paid for this con-firmation if they could afford the test.

Solution 8-50

Thomas and his teammates had played in an afternoon baseball game. After winning, they went to a sports bar to drink and then headed over to a college football game. Thomas was intoxicated and at half time went running onto the field. The crowd yelled obscen-ities him and he got a warning for disorderly conduct.

Solution 8-51

The politician had acciden-tally made plans to attend two engagements, so he sent his twin brother to one of the functions. While there, his twin made some disparaging remarks that several reporters learned of. The politician failed to connect with his brother to find out how the event had gone, and at the press confer-ence he was held accountable for his brother's actions.

Solution 8-52

An Australian company was given the go-ahead to build a cemetery where people could be buried in a vertical posi-tion. This helps to save space and lessen the environmental impact of the graves. Bodies will also be buried in a body bag instead of a casket.

Solution 8-53

He fled from the scene of the

crime, climbed over a nine-foot wall, and found himself in the yard of the city prison.

Solution 8-54

He taught an astronomy class, and as new information about the solar systems and galaxies were discovered, he had to update the material to reflect that. For instance, in May 2005, astronomers discovered twelve new moons orbiting Saturn.

Solution 8-55

The year was 1950, and the salesman had used one of the first Diners Club credit cards to pay for the meal. Diners Club was the original universal credit card (available at more than one location) and was initially available to use at multiple restaurants in New York City. The credit card was marketed to salespeople because of their need to entertain clients.

Solution 8-56

He was an astronaut. On Earth, astronauts will often train in a swimming pool while wearing their spacesuits. This helps to simulate a spacewalk or how to work on equipment.

Solution 8-57

Albert Einstein was awarded the Nobel Prize in Physics in 1921. He was not given the award that year, and instead received the award in 1922 at the same time that Niels Bohr obtained his award for that year.

Solution 8-58

The priest placed a jamming device in his church so that cellular phones would not ring and disturb the members. Unfortunately, when the members could not receive phone calls, they would get up during the service and walk outside to test the reception there.

Solution 8-59

Jordan was a traffic police officer and when he parked his car illegally, which he often did, he left his badge on the dashboard of his vehicle.

Solution 8-60

The business specialized in handicap accessories, and the sign that was made contained the name and store hours. They added Braille to the sign for their blind customers, but the original height was too high for anyone to find and touch.

Solution 9-1

He went walking across a frozen lake. The recent heat wave caused some of the ice to melt and he fell into the water. It froze back over and he wasn't found until the lake unfroze and his body washed ashore.

Solution 9-2

She was a ferret. When a female ferret goes into heat and does not find a mate, she dies.

Solution 9-3

She was drinking gallons of water and died from "water intoxication." In this process, excess water in the body causes sodium levels in the blood to fall. The blood absorbs water and fluid builds up in the brain.

Solution 9-4

She had purchased vertical blinds for her patio door. The doors were quite large, and if she didn't turn them all the way closed, her neighbors could see in from their upstairs bedroom. One night the neighbors heard loud arguing and looked out their window, just in time to see the woman kill her husband in a fit of rage. She attempted to come up with an alibi, but the neighbors testified and she was sentenced to life in prison.

Solution 9-5

Leslie was chopping onions to add to her salad for dinner, and they always made her eyes tear. Her husband came home and stood behind her. He accused her of cheating on him, and when Leslie turned around to deny it, he saw the tears in her eyes. Not realizing what she was cutting, he assumed the tears were signs of guilt and he killed her in a fit of rage.

Solution 9-6

This puzzle is based on Flannery O'Connor's short story "A Good Man Is Hard to Find." The grandmother in the story read a newspaper article about a convicted felon who had escaped from prison. The next day she began a road trip with her son, daughter-in-law, and three grandchildren. The car broke down on a deserted street, and shortly thereafter the felon and his colleagues stopped nearby. The grandmother recognized his face and said his name aloud. The felon and friends then killed the entire family.

Solution 9-7

The father was wealthy and had appointed his oldest son as a patient advocate and durable power of attorney in the event that he went into the hospital and could not make any medical treatment decisions. He knew that if he were on life support, his children would choose to disable

it so they could receive their inheritance more quickly. He attached a codicil to his will in the event that happened. He went into a coma, and days later, his son opted to have the life support removed. The attorney informed the children that all the money was now going to charity.

Solution 9-8

Nadine gave up Hope, her daughter, to her sister's care. Nadine had been struggling with the arguments within her family over who would take care of her young daughter. Once she made the decision, she was at peace, and died shortly thereafter.

Solution 9-9

He had drained an indoor pool and was overcome by the fumes as he repainted it. He passed out and drowned in the few inches of water that remained at the bottom.

Solution 9-10

Nearby kite flyers were having

an "aerial dog fight" competition and were using metallic strings to cut their opponent's kite strings to win the game. One kite was flying low and severed the motorcyclist's head.

Solution 9-11

In this true-life solution, Gary Jackson was arrested after his current girlfriend found an old newspaper clipping he kept tucked in his wallet. The clipping discussed a violent murder and named Jackson as the prime suspect. She called the police, who arrived later to arrest him.

Solution 9-12

The man was charged with evidence tampering after he cut the pacemaker out of his mother's chest. She had died and her son thought that the pacemaker might be evidence against her doctors and the insurance company. He later submitted the pacemaker for a medical examination, and the charges were dropped.

Solution 9-13

She committed suicide so that she could donate her eyes to her two blind sons, hoping that they could undergo surgery and see.

Solution 9-14

In this true incident, the man was a Hindu seer who had announced that he was going to have a spiritually induced death at a specific date and time. When that time came and went, the large crowd became upset and berated him.

Solution 9-15

She lived in China, where the traditional attire for mourning is white. Her husband had recently died and her brothers entered her house wearing all white. When she saw them, she was overcome with grief.

Solution 9-16

He said that her sister had committed suicide by holding her breath. It is impossible to do this. Even if she had tried to hold her breath, she would have developed too much carbon dioxide, lost consciousness, and her body would have begun to breathe again on its own.

Solution 9-17
The dead man was an acquaintance of theirs, and the brothers were hoping to cash in on his pension. They propped the body between them and shuffled into the post office to maneuver his hand onto a fingerprint identification card.

Solution 9-18
He fled, naked, from his burning hunting cabin and was unable to save any of his clothes. He evaded the fire, but froze to death on his snowmobile a few miles away.

Solution 9-19
He was looking for some sympathy votes for an upcoming campaign. He decided to fake an assassination attempt and stabbed his leg to make the attack appear more convincing.

Solution 9-20
The boys did not check the gun chambers, where one bullet resided in each pistol. The first boy to draw and shoot hit a tree. At the same time, the second boy was shooting, but his bullet was on target, killing the first boy instantly.

Solution 9-21
The guard asked his co-worker to stab him through the bulletproof vest to see if it protected him against knife wounds. Unfortunately for the guard, it did not.

Solution 9-22
She shot her husband while he lay in agony, wracked with cancer, on a hospital bed. She thought he only had days to live and did not want to prolong his suffering. Unfortunately, the autopsy reports showed that her husband was cancer-free. He was misdiagnosed, and the pain was due to another illness entirely—one that was treatable.

Solution 9-23

The friends were shooting the beer cans off each other's heads. The first man hit the target correctly. The second man missed, shooting his friend in the face, killing him. The first man was declared the winner of the contest, and the loser when it came to his life.

Solution 9-24

Dave jumped out of the airplane to take aerial photographs of the parachute divers. He forgot to put on his parachute and came crashing to the ground just inches away from where Charlie stood.

Solution 9-25

The woman weighed a couple hundred pounds. Her older, frail husband was following her up the stairs when she slipped and fell. She landed on top of him and he could not move. Neighbors found the couple two days later and he had died as well.

Solution 9-26

He forgot to add the height of his body to the measurement and went crashing into the concrete below.

Solution 9-27

The actor had died performing as a stunt double and the story was featured in the front of the newspaper.

Solution 9-28

The pilots were quickly lifted in an updraft to the top of a cloud. There they acquired a coating of ice and began to fall quickly to the earth below. The ice layer began to melt and refreeze as they passed through the layers of warm and cold air, causing the ice to grow larger around them. Although the parachutes opened, only one man survived the freezing.

Solution 9-29

They were shooting in hot air balloons. Although the bullets missed each other, one bullet struck the balloon, causing it to plunge quickly to the earth below. The man inside died as a result.

Solution 9-30

The victim was enthralled with the mausoleum he was having built and he visited often to ensure that the builders were doing everything correctly. One day he slipped, hit his head on the concrete, and fell into the tomb. He died before the paramedics and police arrived.

Solution 9-31

He had locked his girlfriend out of his house. Instead of going home, she stood in her nightgown calling into the house for him to let her in so they could talk. It was a winter night and the temperature dropped below freezing. The next morning he found her frozen body outside on the porch, and he was later charged with manslaughter.

Solution 9-32

In northwest Pakistan, it is common to serenade the bride with gunfire after a wedding. The groom's kinsmen fire into the air to demonstrate that they are a strong family. Unfortunately, the new weaponry leads to lethal celebrations. In some cases the bullets hit something or ricochet into the crowd.

Solution 9-33

He was working to spray-paint his body orange with hair coloring when he died from inhaling the paint fumes.

Solution 9-34

George had just stolen jewelry and other small valuables from a nearby home when he jumped into the river to evade police. He did not want to part with his goods and kept walking in the river. He slipped and fell, causing his death when he was weighted down to the muddy bottom.

Solution 9-35

Cathy accidentally dropped her purse down an embankment

onto the train tracks as she waited at the subway station. She climbed down to get the purse, but was not able to make it out in time before a train turned the blind corner and killed her instantly.

Solution 9-36
The nurse was taking care of a multiple sclerosis patient who could not feed herself or swallow solid foods. The nurse fed her a piece of bagel and stood by as the patient choked to death.

Solution 9-37
After their child went missing, the parents called the police and then proceeded to drive around the neighborhood themselves. Unbeknown to them, the child had climbed in the trunk and closed the lid. They drove around for hours, and when they arrived home they heard a faint sigh from the trunk. They quickly opened it, but the child died later that evening from heat stroke.

Solution 9-38
The body lay undetected in the bottom of a murky swimming hole until someone saw the head bobbing at the surface. Some of the children who had swum in the hole remembered feeling something at the bottom.

Solution 9-39
Carmen had Steven's cremated remains turned into a round, yellow diamond through a company called LifeGem.

Solution 9-40
Tanya was an overprotective mother hippo, and she smothered ten of her fifteen babies.

Solution 9-41
In this true story, Ryoko Ishida was a freshman when she was tardy for the first time. She entered the schoolyard as one of the teachers slammed the 500-pound iron gate shut. The teacher was there, determined to discourage late students. Ryoko was crushed against the wall by

the gate, and died a couple of hours later.

Solution 9-42

Tommy sat down on the couch next to James to reason with him. When James fired the gun at his own head, the bulleted exited and killed Tommy as well.

Solution 9-43

In 1987, Roh Ki Hwa of South Korea forgot to change her watch to adjust for daylight saving time. She went on a walk with her daughter and returned two hours later to the picnic she and her husband were attending. She had not prepared her husband's noon meal and was deeply embarrassed. Hwa hung herself in her home.

Solution 9-44

In Northern Europe as late as 1545, it was considered immodest to hang or burn women. When hanging, their skirts could billow up in the wind. When burning, the fire would first burn their clothes and expose their bodies to the masses. So instead, when convicted of a crime, women were buried alive.

Solution 9-45

In this true story, Rachel Haigh from Hastings, England, was rushed to the hospital after complaining of stomach pains. Physicians found a large hairball that filled her stomach cavity. She suffered internal bleeding after the surgery and died in the hospital.

Solution 9-46

The friends decided to throw a firecracker into the lake to kill the fish and send them to the surface. Unfortunately, their boat drifted over the dynamite and was damaged heavily during the explosion. One man drowned, but his friend made it safely to shore.

Solution 9-47

He climbed in the airplane wheel well in an attempt to escape his country. He died of frostbite during the flight and fell to the ground when the landing gear was deployed.

Solution 9-48

The bird was carrying a snake, which managed to escape the bird's grasp. The snake landed in the vehicle and bit one of the passengers, a child, before the others could kill it. The poisonous venom killed the child before they could reach a hospital.

Solution 9-49

The Practitioner, a British medical journal, determined that bird-watching may be hazardous to a person's health. They documented this when a bird-watcher died from a crocodile attack. He was so absorbed in what he was watching that he was unaware of his surroundings, and a crocodile devoured him.

Solution 9-50

He shot himself while skydiving. When he dropped the gun, it fell thousands of feet

and was embedded over a foot underground.

Solution 9-51

Isadora Duncan, a famous American dancer, was wearing a long, silk scarf when she took a drive that evening. As she climbed into the car, one loose end of the scarf fell over the side of the car and wrapped around the rear axle. As the car sped away, the scarf tightened and pulled Duncan over the side. She was strangled and killed instantly.

Solution 9-52

The prisoner literally killed himself by swallowing the only thing allowed in his cell, a pocket-sized Bible.

Solution 9-53

The woman cut her toe, nicking a vein, while giving herself a pedicure. She walked around looking for a towel to staunch the bleeding and clean up the mess. She ultimately bled to death. If she had stayed still and kept her foot elevated, the bleeding might have stopped.

ants in her stomach. She poisoned herself.

Solution 9-54

The magician fell down in the middle of his show and died instantly from a heart attack. Members of the audience thought it was part of the act and cheered him on.

Solution 9-55

The thief stole the collection money from the church and ran outside into the street. A bus accidentally ran him over and he died from the injuries. Those in the congregation felt God had struck him down for his crime.

Solution 9-56

Laurie left her house in a rush and had to apply her make-up in the car. She was putting on her lipstick when she braked suddenly and choked on the tube.

Solution 9-57

She ran inside and swallowed some insecticide to kill the

Solution 9-58

The woman was afraid of being unhappy, so she committed suicide before that could happen.

Solution 9-59

Frank had just learned that the company who was supposed to have cremated his wife's body had, in fact, given him an urn full of soil. The crematorium was not burning the bodies because the machine had shut down. For many years, they just buried the bodies or threw them in a lake. Frank's wife's body was found and he wanted to exchange the urn in her plot at the cemetery with her ashes.

Solution 10-1

He was a dragonfly, and the dragonfly's average lifespan is approximately 24 hours.

Solution 10-2

She was looking for crocodile

dung. Ancient Egyptians, around 1850 B.C., created contraceptive diaphragms made of crocodile dung, honey, and sodium carbonate.

Solution 10-3

She listened to the crickets. It is said that if you count the number of chirps for fifteen seconds and add 37 degrees, the result will be close to the actual temperature in Fahrenheit. Other sources say to count for thirteen minutes and add 40 degrees, or count for one minute, subtract 40, divide by four, and add 50.

Solution 10-4

He was a male emperor moth. The males can smell a female emperor moth from seven miles away.

Solution 10-5

She was in China, where in some areas citizens add salt to their tea instead of sugar.

Solution 10-6

She made him eat spinach, as it was touted as a vegetable with a high amount of iron and he was anemic. In actuality, spinach has no more iron than any other vegetable. In 1870, Dr. E. von Wolf incorrectly calculated the amount of iron in spinach. He put his decimal point in the wrong place, suggesting that spinach had an iron count ten times higher than it actually did.

Solution 10-7

Sally was Jane's pregnant goldfish, and they are also called "twits."

Solution 10-8

Because natural gas has no smell, gas companies add trace amounts of mercaptan, an odorant that smells like rotten eggs. This helps patrons easily detect a gas leak in their home.

Solution 10-9

Earlier in the testimony, she said that as the accused left her house, she saw a rainbow outside in the distance. When she later said that he had left around noon, the attorney knew she was lying. Rainbows can only be seen in the morning or late afternoon when the sun is behind you. The sun must be less than 40 degrees above the horizon.

Solution 10-10
It was 1999 and the child brought in stamps that had been printed by the post office. The stamps contained a picture of the Grand Canyon and the incorrect message "Grand Canyon, Colorado."

Solution 10-11
Janice was a butterfly, and her taste receptors are in her feet so that she can quickly locate nectar in blossoms.

Solution 10-12
Louise is an elephant, and they are pregnant for two years. She became pregnant in late 1999 and gave birth in 2001.

Solution 10-13
Jeremy and Joshua were birds. Birds cannot swallow without gravity, so they slowly starved to death.

Solution 10-14
Kevin owned twenty racehorses. Arbitrarily, all racehorses in the northern hemisphere celebrate their birthday on January 1, regardless of when in the year they were born.

Solution 10-15
There was a complete solar eclipse. The temperature can drop by 6 degrees Celsius (about 20 degrees Fahrenheit).

Solution 10-16
He's a flamingo, and they turn from gray to pink when they eat plankton and shrimp.

Solution 10-17
They were cats that help to guard and protect Russian artwork at the Hermitage museum in St. Petersburg. They've been a part of the "security" system since Catherine the Great started the collection in 1764. She brought in selected cats to try to keep the building rodent-free, and today there are approximately fifty cats

who live in the museum basement. They are barred from the exhibit halls so they don't disturb the artwork.

Solution 10-18

She was a seahorse. In the world of seahorses, the female inserts ripe eggs into the male's brood pouch. The male then fertilizes the eggs and carries them for approximately three weeks before giving birth to live seahorse babies.

Solution 10-19

It is the planet Venus. Venus has a dense cloud layer and it reflects nearly all of the sunlight it receives, making it very visible when you look out at the night sky.

Solution 10-20

He was a South American Indian heading off to a tribal war. He captured a local Poison Dart Frog (also known as a Dendrobate) and rubbed the tips of his blow darts onto the frog's back. The frog secretes a toxin from its skin that can cause death in humans and animals.

Solution 10-21

He was traveling from Juneau to Nome, Alaska. Although the state is spread over four time zones, the government compressed three of the time zones into one in order to improve business and communication. This means that in parts of the year the sun is overhead in Juneau at 3:00 P.M. instead of noon.

Solution 10-22

Martha took the dog with her because he was a seizure-alert dog. She suffered from epileptic seizures and he could detect a seizure in advance of the attack. He was also trained to stay with her to keep her safe during the attack, or to go get help.

Solution 10-23

John always ate his cereal with a sliced banana on top. His mom had recently read that mosquitoes are more attracted to a human who has recently eaten a banana. Since John was allergic to mosquito bites, she wanted to deter as many mosquitoes as possible since he was going on a camping trip and would be surrounded by the insects.

Solution 10-24
It was August 2, 1922, and the United States phone service was shut down for one minute during the funeral of telephone inventor Alexander Graham Bell.

Solution 10-25
She was an astronaut and in the space shuttle during a mission. The tears formed in her eyes and then broke free to float around the shuttle.

Solution 10-26
The words were inscribed on the first penny minted with the words "United States of America." The year was 1727.

Solution 10-27
At the end of the second side of the album Sgt. Pepper by the Beatles, there is a high-pitched ultrasonic dog whistle. The group added the sound after a conversation about wavelengths that they had with their engineer. When the album was played, Cassie's dog would howl at the whistle.

Solution 10-28
Every fourteen years the Earth passes through the same plane as the rings on Saturn, meaning that Saturn shows its rings edge-on. The rings are thin and disappear from view to all but the most powerful telescopes. Percy did not see the rings and thought Saturn was a different planet.

Solution 10-29
They were paid a salary. The word salary derives from the Latin "salarium," which was money given to Roman soldiers to purchase salt for seasoning and food preservation.

Solution 10-30
She had a wound that wasn't healing properly. She had

heard that Blowfly maggots are often used to treat patients with infections. The maggots eat the dead tissue and get rid of harmful bacteria. Over 200 hospitals in the United States and Europe use maggots and about 5,000 laboratory-grown maggots are delivered each week.

Solution 10-31

It is the longest word in the English language that has all of the letters in alphabetical order.

Solution 10-32

It is one of the longest words where the six vowels (including y) are in alphabetical order.

Solution 10-33

It is one of the longest words composed entirely of letters that have horizontal symmetry when written in upper case.

Solution 10-34

It is one of the longest words that can be typed alternating between each hand.

Solution 10-35

It is one of the longest words that has 180-degree rotational symmetry.

Solution 10-36

It is the only state name with one syllable.

Solution 10-37

It can be pronounced at least seven different ways, including the sounds made in these words: tough, dough, plough, cough, hiccough, through, and wrought.

Solution 10-38

The symbol (#), like the button on your phone.

Solution 10-39

It is the only Roman capital letter with only one endpoint.

Solution 10-40

It is the only letter that does not yet appear anywhere on the periodic table of the elements.

Solution 10-41

It is the word with the highest

amount of definitions—464 in the Oxford dictionary.

Solution 10-42
Run zig-zag. A crocodile has a hard time making sharp turns.

Solution 10-43
The common housefly is the most dangerous, because it transmits more diseases than any other animal. The housefly picks up contamination from feces and passes it when it lands on your food or drink.

Solution 10-44
They are the names of the three monkeys (see no evil, hear no evil, speak no evil). In Japanese, the names are translated into mizaru, kikazaru, and iwazaru. The word for monkey, "saru," has the same sound as the verb-ending "zaru," so the origin of the monkeys may be a play on words.

Solution 10-45
It is one of the most frequently misspelled words.

Solution 10-46
They are the names of the two thieves crucified with Jesus.

Solution 10-47
Flammable. Flammable and inflammable both mean easily ignited and capable of burning rapidly. Most companies use the term "flammable" when it comes to warning consumers of products, since many people view the prefix -in as meaning "not."

Solution 10-48
A blue whale vocalizes as loud as 188 decibels and can be heard as far as 530 miles away.

Solution 10-49
Six. Ernest Hemingway is quoted as having penned the most effective shortest story as "For Sale: Baby Shoes. Never Used."

Solution 10-50
Jaws.

Solution 10-51
It is one of the longest words

that can be played on an instrument using music notes.

Solution 10-52
Treasure Island.

Solution 10-53
It is the longest word in the English language where all of the letters in the word are in reverse alphabetical order.

Solution 10-54
Of Mice and Men.

Solution 10-55
It is the longest word that can be written such that the reader cannot tell if it has been written in uppercase or lowercase letters.

Solution 10-56
Gone With the Wind.

Solution 10-57
Phobophobia.

Solution 10-58
It is one of many ten-letter words that can be typed using only the top row of keys.

Solution 10-59
It is the only 15-letter word that can be spelled without repeating a letter.

Solution 11-1
The numbers represent the number of letters in each month starting with January (7). The sixth month is June and has 4 letters.

Solution 11-2
t. If you look across the top row of a standard keyboard and alternate letters, the keys on the row are q, e, t, u, o, [.

Solution 11-3
6. The numbers represent the numeric representation of the first letter in each day of the week starting with Sunday (S = 19th letter of the alphabet). The sixth day is Friday (F = 6).

Solution 11-4
1. The numbers represent the numeric equivalent to the letters in the word "alphabet." The fifth letter is a (1).

Solution 11-5
D. The sequence contains the second letter of the last names of the Presidents of the United

States in chronological order. The second President was John Adams.

Solution 11-6

22. The sequence contains the numeric representation of the first letter of the astrological signs in order, starting with Aries (1). The sixth astrological sign is Virgo (22).

Solution 11-7

10. The sequence contains the numeric equivalent of the first letter of the books of the Bible in order, starting with Genesis (7). The sixth book of the Bible is Joshua (10).

Solution 11-8

5. The numbers represent the number of letters in each of the planets in our solar system, starting from Mercury (7) and working outward. The third planet is Earth and has 5 letters.

Solution 11-9

6. The numbers represent the number of letters in each color of the rainbow starting with red (3). The third color is yellow and has 6 letters.

Solution 11-10

C. The sequence contains the first letter of the last name of the Democratic Presidential nominees starting from the 2004 elections with John Kerry (K) and working back through Al Gore, William Clinton, Michael Dukakis, and finally Jimmy Carter (C).

Solution 11-11

W. The sequence contains the first letter of the character, in order, of the tales in Geoffrey Chaucer's Canterbury Tales. The first tale was the Knight (K), followed by the Miller, the Reeve, the Cook, the Man of Law, and sixth was the Wife of Bath (W).

Solution 11-12

S. The series contains the first letter in the periods in the geological timescale, starting from creation and moving toward today. The first period was the Cambrian (C), followed by Ordovician, Silurian (S), Devonian, Carboniferous, and Permian.

Solution 11-13

8. The sequence represents the number of letters in each state of the United States, in alphabetical order from Alabama (7), through Colorado (8).

Solution 11-14

8. The numbers represent the number of letters in each capital of the United States, in alphabetical order from Albany (7), through Bismarck (8).

Solution 11-15

7. The numbers in this sequence correspond to the numeric equivalent for the first letters of the colors in the rainbow—starting with red (18). The fourth color is green (7).

Solution 11-16

S. The letters are the first letter of each word in this puzzle "What comes next in this sequence."

Solution 11-17

Ne. The letters read across the periodic table of the elements starting with Boron (B) and ending with Neon (Ne).

Solution 11-18

d. The letters start from the beginning of the alphabet and work upward. The lowercase letters represent their respective uppercase letters and each uppercase letter contains at least one curved line.

Solution 11-19

black. The colors represent the order of the standard belt system in karate. Some schools have introduced blue, orange, and purple into the system, but the standard five colors are as they appear in the puzzle.

Solution 11-20

Sherman. The list contains the last name of Chicago mayors in chronological order since 1837.

Solution 11-21

e. The sequence contains the

first letters of the words of modern birthstones for each month starting from April.

Solution 11-22
a. The list contains the first letters of the words of anniversary gemstones starting with the second wedding anniversary—garnet, pearl, topaz, sapphire, amethyst.

Solution 11-23
A. The sequence contains the first letters of the continents in order of size (square kilometers), from highest to lowest: Asia, Africa, North America, South America, Antarctica.

Solution 11-24
SA. The sequence contains the first letters of the continents in order of population size, from highest to lowest: Asia, Africa, Europe, North America, South America.

Solution 11-25
A. The sequence contains the continents in order of the number of countries they contain,

from highest to lowest: Africa, Europe, Asia, North America, Australia-Oceania.

Solution 11-26
Madagascar. The sequence contains the major islands in order of size (square kilometers), from highest to lowest.

Solution 11-27
Czech Republic. The list corresponds to the youngest countries, starting with the youngest (East Timor in 2002).

Solution 11-28
Huron. The sequence refers to the major streets encountered when traveling north on Michigan Avenue from the Chicago River in Chicago.

Solution 11-29
Vermont. The sequence corresponds to the names of states in properties when starting from GO on the classic monopoly board.

Solution 11-30
d. The sequence corresponds to the music notes played

in "London Bridge Is Falling Down."

Solution 11-31

African American. The list contains the top United States ancestries by population, starting with German.

Solution 11-32

Non-natural disaster. The list contains the top costly disasters as stated by the International Federation of Red Cross and Red Cross Societies.

Solution 11-33

Mercedes. The list contains the top best-selling global brands as stated by Interbrand.

Solution 11-34

Ross. The list contains the top islands by elevation.

Solution 11-35

Oak Grove. The list contains the most common United States cities by name.

Solution 11-36

d. The sequence contains the names of polygons going upward in number of sides starting with pentagon (p) and ending with decagon (d).

Solution 11-37

s. The sequence is the order of "calling in the directions" in various rituals. The process begins with the four directions (north, east, south, west), and then calls in "above" and "below."

Solution 11-38

10. The sequence refers to the price (in cents) of postage stamps required to send a one-ounce envelope, starting in 1885.

Solution 11-39

L. The sequence corresponds to the Group 1 elements in the periodic table, starting with Hydrogen and ending with Francium. The Group 1 elements are those with one electron in their outer shell.

Solution 11-40

15. The sequence contains the numeric equivalent to the first letter in the names of The Great Lakes, from west to east.

Solution 11-41

16. The sequence contains the numeric equivalent to the first letter in the movie rating system: G, PG, PG-13, R, NC-17.

Solution 11-42

M. The sequence contains the first letter of the names of the American states, in the order that they joined the Union.

Solution 11-43

nurse. The sequence contains the first several characters from the "Farmer in the Dell."

Solution 11-44

three. The sequence consists of the first word in each line in the lyrics "Blue Suede Shoes," words and music written by Carl Perkins.

Solution 11-45

E. The series contains the first letter of the titles in British Isles nobility (male), in order from highest (Duke) to lowest (Baron). The third title is Earl.

Solution 11-46

s. The sequence refers to the Spanish numbers—uno, dos, tres, cuatro, cinco, seis, siete.

Solution 11-47

s. The series contains the words starting with "whole" and dividing by two each time—whole, half, quarter, eighth, sixteenth.

Solution 11-48

P. The sequence contains the first letters of the United States time zones, starting with Atlantic Standard Time, and working west to Hawaii-Aleutian Standard Time.

Solution 11-49

H. The series corresponds to the first letter in the menu choices across the top of a Microsoft Windows toolbar.

Solution 11-50

A. The sequence contains the first letter in the Maslow's Hierarchy of needs in psychology—Physiological, Safety, Love/Belonging, Esteem, Actualization.

Solution 11-51
L. This sequence contains the first initials of the Jackson children, including Michael Jackson. The fifth child born was LaToya.

Solution 11-52
C. The series includes the first letter in the names of the Galilean moons, in order of their orbit. The last moon is Callisto.

Solution 11-53
s. The list contains the first letters of the words in Aristotle's six parts of a tragedy—plot, character, thought/theme, diction, music/melody, and spectacle.

Solution 11-54
k. The sequence corresponds to the first letter of the names of the chesspieces in the back row, starting with rook and moving to king. The second piece is the knight.

Solution 11-55
D. The series is the positions you move your shift lever through when driving an automatic transmission automobile, starting with Park and moving through to 2nd. The fourth position is Drive (D).

Solution 11-56
SF. This list contains the first letters of each word, ranking high to low, in winning hands of poker: Royal Flush (RF), Straight Flush (SF), Four of a Kind (FK), Full House (FH), Flush (FL), Straight (ST), Three of a Kind (TK), Two Pair (TP).

Solution 11-57
e. The sequence contains the second letter of the Greek name of each of the letters in the Greek alphabet—alpha, beta, gamma, delta, epsilon, zeta, eta.

Solution 11-58
e. This puzzle lists the atmospheric layers, starting from the troposphere (t) and moving outward to the exosphere (e).

Solution 11-59
L. The series consists of the Erik Erikson's eight develop-

mental stages (psychosocial stages) starting with Infancy, Toddler, Early Childhood, Elementary/Middle School Years, Adolescence, Young Adulthood, Middle Adulthood, and Late Adulthood.

Solution 11-60

f. This puzzle simply lists the first letters of the words "fifth, fourth, third, second, and first."

Solution 12-1

apple. The remaining words are all contained in the "Twelve Days of Christmas" lyrics.

Solution 12-2

Ketchup. Ketchup is the only flavor of the group that Baskin Robbins made into an ice cream.

Solution 12-3

California. Each of the other states contains a city of the same name.

Solution 12-4

pale. The other four words can be typed using only your left hand on a keyboard.

Solution 12-5

Rome. Unlike the other cities, there is a city named Rome on every continent.

Solution 12-6

door. The other words use the short vowel sounds.

Solution 12-7

parrot. The remaining animals were all pets of the Kennedy family when John F. Kennedy was president.

Solution 12-8

loyal. The other words are all names of car models made by various automobile companies.

Solution 12-9

sofa. If you replace the last letter of the other words with the letter "e", the new words all exist in the dictionary.

Solution 12-10

trade. If you remove the letter "r" from the other words, the remaining letters still form a word in the dictionary.

Solution 12-11
Daniel. The other names have been the most popular male baby name for at least one year since 1950, according to the Social Security Administration.

Solution 12-12
purple. The other colors are used for major street signs.

Solution 12-13
r. The other letters, when writing them as uppercase instead of lowercase, only use straight lines.

Solution 12-14
giraffe. The other words are symbols in the astrological signs of the zodiac.

Solution 12-15
jealous. The other words are synonyms for the names of dwarfs in *Snow White and the Seven Dwarves*.

Solution 12-16
time. The other words are contained in the bagua symbol of feng shui.

Solution 12-17
teddy. The other toys are in the extended lyrics of the Christmas carol "Santa Claus Is Coming to Town."

Solution 12-18
Romeo. Although all five of these are Shakespearean characters, Romeo is the only one who was not a king.

Solution 12-19
apple. The remaining words were all included in the names of the original Crayola box of 64 crayons.

Solution 12-20
elephant. The other animals are members of the Chinese Zodiac.

Solution 12-21
sofa. If the word "The" is placed in front of the remaining words, they form stories in the *Grimm's Complete Fairy Tales*.

Solution 12-22
Jasper. The other words are some of the brightest stars seen from Earth.

Solution 12-23
energy. The remaining words are all flavors of teabags offered by Tazo Tea.

Solution 12-24
Ohio. The rest are members of the top five states with the highest population.

Solution 12-25
New York. The rest are members of the top five states in the United States with the largest area.

Solution 12-26
Florida. The remaining states contain cities within the top five highest populations.

Solution 12-27
Tim. The remaining names are characters that Humphrey Bogart has played.

Solution 12-28
Toronto. The other cities have hosted the summer Olympics since 1896.

Solution 12-29
Switzerland. The remaining countries are all members of NATO (North Atlantic Treaty Organization).

Solution 12-30
The Great Gatsby. Francis Ford Coppola directed the other films. He was a writer for *The Great Gatsby*, but did not direct it.

Solution 12-31
dance. The remaining words are all names of National Basketball Association (NBA) teams.

Solution 12-32
eyeglasses. The other words are the titles of short stories written by Stephen King.

Solution 12-33
pirate. The remaining words are all the names of United States National Parks.

Solution 12-34
Chrysler is the only company that has not been listed in the Fortune 100.

Solution 12-35
kite. If you add an s to the beginning and end of the

remaining words, they form new words.

Solution 12-36

poor. If you spell the remaining words backwards, they form new words.

Solution 12-37

crime. The remaining words are autoantonyms—single words that have meanings that contradict each other.

Solution 12-38

condors. The other words are all names of National Football League (NFL) teams.

Solution 12-39

choir. The remaining words are all names of Edgar Allen Poe works.

Solution 12-40

humphead wrasse. The other endangered animals have been released back into the wild.

Solution 12-41

sing. The other words have homonyms—words that are pronounced the same but have different spellings and meanings. In this puzzle, the homonyms are band and banned, aisle and isle, chants and chance, choir and quire.

Solution 12-42

bulb. The remaining words are eponyms—words derived from people's names.

Solution 12-43

display. The remaining choices are homographs—words that are spelled the same but have different meanings and pronunciations. In this puzzle, minute could have a definition of "60 seconds" or "tiny."

Solution 12-44

travel. The other words are the names of horses that have won the Kentucky Derby.

Solution 12-45

Hudson. The remaining words are names of NASA space missions.

Solution 12-46

cat. The domestic cat is mentioned nowhere in the Bible. The other animals here are mentioned multiple times.

Solution 12-47
skip. If you add "ful" to the end of the remaining words, they form new words.

Solution 12-48
Treasure. The remaining words are all titles of Rudyard Kipling poems.

Solution 12-49
key. The other words are used in various superstitions.

Solution 12-50
Ireland. This is the only country not in the same time zone as the other countries.

Solution 12-51
planet. The other objects are included in at least one of the United States state flags.

Solution 12-52
cake. The other words are derived by taking one or more of the first and last letters of a state to make a word. Man is from "MichigAN," vent is from "VErmoNT," key is from "KEntuckY," etc.

Solution 12-53
taste. The others are all names of the original nine Ty Beanie Babies.

Solution 12-54
double. The remaining words are all terms used by winemakers as they weigh and measure the wine.

Solution 12-55
castle. The other words are names of tarot cards in the Major Arcana.

Solution 12-56
beach. The remaining choices are the titles of Woody Allen movies.

Solution 12-57
tall. The remaining choices are all adjectives that cannot be compared (should not be used with the words more, most, less, least, or with endings –er or –est).

Solution 12-58
goods. The other words are all nouns ending in "s" that are commonly singular. They

appear to be plural nouns, but are treated as singular and used with a singular verb.

Solution 12-59
silver. This word does not rhyme with any other word in the English dictionary.

Solution 12-60
chair. First notice boot and fall—together, they anagram to football. Similarly, you can put sin and net together to make tennis, and balk and stable to make basketball. This leaves chair as the odd word.

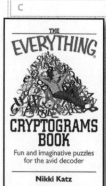

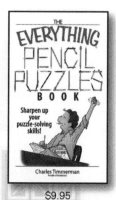